Classroom Management from to A Z

Robert T. Tauber

Associate Professor of Education
Pennsylvania State University

Classroom Management from A to Z

Holt, Rinehart and Winston, Inc.
Fort Worth   Chicago   San Francisco   Philadelphia
Montreal   Toronto   London   Sydney   Tokyo

Publisher: Ted Buchholz
Acquisitions Editor: Jo-Anne Weaver
Senior Project Editor: Dawn Youngblood
Production Manager: Ken Dunaway
Art & Design Supervisor: Vicki McAlindon Horton
Text Designer: Jo Carol Arnold/Arnold Studio
Cover Designer: Jo Carol Arnold/Arnold Studio

Library of Congress Cataloging-in-Publication Data
Tauber, Robert T.
  Classroom management from A to Z / Robert T. Tauber.
    p.   cm.
  Bibliography: p.
  Includes index.
  ISBN 0-03-030003-7
    1. Classroom management—United States.   2. School discipline
—United States.   I. Title.
LB3011.T38   1990
371.1'024—dc20   89-15474

ISBN: 0-03- -030003-7

Address Editorial Correspondence To: 301 Commerce Street, Suite 3700
                                        Fort Worth, TX 76102
                   Address Orders To: 6277 Sea Harbor Drive, Orlando, FL 32887
                                        1-800-782-4479, or 1-800-433-0001 (in Florida)

Printed in the United States of America

0 1 2 3   090   9 8 7 6 5 4 3 2 1

Holt, Rinehart and Winston, Inc.
The Dryden Press
Saunders College Publishing

Copyright acknowledgments follow index.

TEXTBOOK DESIGN AND ORGANIZATION

This book on classroom management has four chapters. Chapter I is relatively short, but provides some up-front, straight talk about discipline. Please read it; it sets the stage and tone for what follows.

Chapter II runs through the alphabet with briefly presented "A" through "Z" suggestions for improving classroom discipline. Individually, the application of the suggestions CAN improve classroom discipline. Collectively, the application of a majority of the suggestions WILL improve classroom discipline. Further reading on selective suggestions is encouraged via cited references. Use the suggestions; they work.

Chapter III identifies concepts in discipline that may have been under-presented, incorrectly presented, or overlooked completely in prior coursework. These are presented in more detail than the suggestions in Chapter II. I believe that classroom teachers interested in improving classroom management must be aware of the material presented in Chapter III—for example, Social Bases of Power, Negative Reinforcement (not to be confused with Punishment), Body Language, Defusing Power Struggles, and Self-Fulfilling Prophecy.

Finally, Chapter IV briefly describes the *Educational Resources Information Center* (ERIC) system for quickly and inexpensively retrieving additional information on *any* aspect of classroom discipline. There simply is no better vehicle available to educators for getting the information they need whether related to their field, in general, or to classroom management, in particular. Available for over twenty years now, it is one of the best-kept secrets in education.

There is no Chapter V—or summarizing chapter. By the time the reader has completed Chapter IV, there is little left to say. If the Chapter I "peptalk" has been successful, the reader will have gone on to read and, hopefully, use the meat of this book—Chapters II and III. Further, if Chapter IV accomplishes its objective, the reader will have put down the book and scurried off to the nearest college/university library to conduct a search of classroom management topics most closely related to the reader's unique set of circumstances. What would be the purpose of a concluding Chapter V?

One might wonder why Chapter II, an application-oriented chapter, preceeds Chapter III, a more theory-oriented chapter. I believe the current arrangement is more useful to busy and/or new practitioners. The book builds the reader's involvement from a "let's convince the reader that classroom management is worth studying" Chapter I, to a "here are some concrete, practical suggestions" Chapter II, to a "let's delve further into specific theories" Chapter III, to a "here is how you learn more about what may be missing from this book" Chapter IV. Further, sufficient cross-referencing is made between Chapters II and III.

One might also wonder why Chapter IV was not simply included as an appendix. Fewer people would read it if it were relegated to the status of

"Appendix." Chapter IV needs to be read—needs to be used. Chapter IV recognizes that no one book can have all possible information on the subject of classroom management. But ERIC, as a resource understood and used by educators, *can get that information.* Thus, this book is powerful beyond its covers. The reader would be shortchanged by reducing the visibility of ERIC—a tool related to effective classroom management.

WHO SHOULD USE THIS BOOK?

This book is meant to be used by those who do not have, at the moment, the time to read lots of theory-based articles and books on discipline. Among those most likely to benefit from this book area:

1. college students taking part in early off campus, in-the-school, field experiences. Increasingly, these experiences are being required by state and regional certification bodies.
2. students taking an educational psychology course, where the primary text may devote, at best, just one chapter to classroom management.
3. student teachers who are taking part in a semester-long practicum, where effective classroom management skills are a must, not a luxury.
4. first- and second-year classroom teachers who, like their student teacher counterparts, need effective classroom management skills for success—perhaps even survival.
5. teachers taking part in ever-increasing state-mandated induction year programs.
6. seasoned teachers who may not have had sufficient course work in the area of classroom management *or* who simply wish quickly to review the area of discipline.

While this book has been written with the busy educator in mind, at the same time, the suggestions in Chapter II, as well as the slightly longer presentations in Chapter III, are *all* based upon theory. It is for this very reason that the classroom management strategies described are effective in the first place.

AUDIENCES OUTSIDE OF EDUCATION

Although this book is written primarily for those in teacher training and for classroom teachers, preschool through high school, its usefulness does not stop there. The "A" through "Z" suggestions in Chapter II, the slightly longer articles in Chapter III, and ERIC in Chapter IV are definitely applicable to other situations where one finds himself/herself responsible for teaching others. Consider using these management skills as a Boy

Scout, Girl Scout, Cub Scout or Brownie leader. Here we have adults, with all the proper motivation to want to teach young people, who are often ill-equipped to do the job for which they have volunteered.

Consider the application of these classroom management skills by Sunday school teachers of children and adolescents, as well as by volunteers at local YMCAs and YWCAs and other youth groups. In each of these cases, the adult is responsible for "keeping the learning act afloat." Classroom management skills play a key role in providing you more time to teach *and* your students more time to learn.

Another very important—perhaps the most important—category of adults who could profit by using the material in this book is parents. They, too, must keep the "learning act afloat." They are the child's first teachers, first youth group leaders, first almost everything!

No topic in either Chapter II or Chapter III will take more than a few pages to present. Each classroom management suggestion is presented, explained, and defended. Where appropriate, selected references for further reading are offered. That's it. That's all one needs to get started on more effective classroom management strategies.

R.T.T.

I wish to acknowledge the help that many people have given toward the development of this book. First and foremost, I would like to thank my Educational Psychology students who, through their many hours in off campus field experiences in local schools, have been able, by means of their questions and comments, to help me identify and refine my suggestions for classroom management. I am indebted to the principals, superintendents, student teacher supervisors, and fellow educational psychology faculty who have read the initial drafts of the book and made subsequent suggestions. A special thanks is offered to Mrs. Wendy Eidenmuller, who willingly read and marked drafts of this book. Without her input, this book would not have been possible. I wish to thank my wife, Cecelia, and my children, David and Rebecca, for allowing me the evenings and weekends away from my family that were needed to complete this project. Finally, I want to thank my parents, Katherine and Thomas, for their lifelong encouragement for this, as well as for any and all other projects.

R.T.T.

CHAPTER I Some Straight Talk on Discipline   1

This chapter is designed to help the reader recognize the need for classroom management skills, to put such skills into the larger perspective of keeping the learning act afloat, and to appreciate the present state of affairs regarding the teaching of such skills, that is, the lack of required classroom management coursework in teacher training programs.

CHAPTER II "A" Through "Z" Suggestions   13

Chapter II consists of concrete suggestions that, when implemented, will help teachers establish *and* maintain effective classroom management. Each suggestion has a theoretical base.

**CHAPTER III Selected Articles on
Aspects of Classroom Management**   79

A series of short articles addresses selected classroom management skills and theories that are often overlooked or have been incorrectly presented in prior course work. It is hard to conceive of a teacher establishing and/or maintaining effective classroom management without a working knowledge of the material presented in this chapter.

Classroom
Management
from
A to Z

Some Straight Talk on Discipline

DISCIPLINE: A REAL PROBLEM?

The "Annual Gallup Poll of the Public's Attitudes Toward the Public Schools," published regularly in the September issue of *Phi Delta Kappan,* has, for almost two decades, identified "Lack of Discipline" as one of the biggest problems with which the public schools must deal. In fact, "Lack of Discipline" has been singled out as the number one problem more often than any other.

Do teachers see "the discipline problem" differently than the public does? Not according to "The Second Gallup/Phi Delta Kappa Poll of Teachers' Attitudes Toward the Public Schools" (Elam 1989). Fifty percent of the surveyed elementary and secondary teachers describe today's discipline problem as either "very serious" or "fairly serious." When asked why teachers leave the profession, forty-three percent cited "discipline problems in schools." Classroom management strategies, a more palatable way of saying "discipline," clearly need some attention!

What Is Your Philosophy of Discipline?

It has been my experience that at least two questions regularly are asked by principals of those applying for teaching jobs. "What is your philosophy of discipline?" and "What is your philosophy of education?" Actually, the two go hand in hand, the latter being a prerequisite for the former. The point is, though, that those asking the questions are often thankful that they don't have to answer the questions. Just as it is the case that today's education graduates have had little in the way of training (education) concerning classroom management techniques, so it is also true for graduates of yesteryear—today's senior teachers and administrators. One may get lucky and find a mentor who can pass on effective, as well as constitutionally legal, techniques of discipline. But what if you don't? Read on.

What Is Your Philosophy of Education?

I am not sure those asking this question really are more interested in receiving an answer or simply in seeing how you will respond under pressure while trying to answer. After all, who is going to say anything but something suggesting

respect for "individual student differences," assuming an obligation to
help all students reach their "potential," promoting "good citizenship,"
and the like?

Actually, a good deal of thought should be given to your philosophy of
education. Wolfgang and Glickman (1980, 1986), fearful that the word
"philosophy" would scare away readers, substituted the terminology
"school of thought." So, what is your school of thought regarding how
students learn, develop, and grow?

Basically, teachers are either Interventionists, Noninterventionists, or
Interactionalists. According to Wolfgang and Glickman (1980, 1986),
Interventionists believe that children develop according to environmental
conditions. You as a classroom teacher are one of those conditions. A
teacher's job is to control the environment by implementing a logical system of conditioning. "By accepting a position as a teacher, a person has
not only the right but an 'obligation' to modify student behavior" (Axelrod
1977, p. 158). Here we find proponents of the "carrot-and-stick" approach. Here we find operant conditioning, behavior modification, and
shaping as some of many relied upon concepts. The teacher is in the
forefront. Canter and Canter's *Assertive Discipline* (1976), Dobson's *Dare
to Discipline* (1970), and B. F. Skinner's thinking fit here.

Noninterventionists believe in providing a supportive, facilitating
environment for students. There is a faith that the student possesses an
internal motivation which, if simply nurtured (not controlled), will blos-
som. Like the flower that requires only nurturing water, soil, and sunlight
to bloom, so, too, the capacity for a child's growth is dependent upon that
child, not a controlling teacher. The child simply requires a correct
environment to bloom. Although the teacher, better called director or
facilitator, is no longer in the forefront, this is not a laissez faire, complete
hands-off view as some may assume. The concepts in Gordon's *Parent
Effectiveness Training* (1970) and *Teacher Effectiveness Training*
(1974) and Rogers' *Freedom to Learn* (1969) fit here.

Interactionalists believe that "conflicts cannot be resolved without
shared responsibility, without full participation in decision making by all
the participants in a conflict" (Dreikurs and Cassel 1972, p. 71). It takes
two to cause a problem, and it takes two to solve it. What is important to
interactionalists is not how many conflicts occur, but how those conflicts
are resolved so that relationships remain intact; both parties save face and
feel their needs have been met. See Glasser's *Schools Without Failure*
(1969), and Dreikurs and Cassel's *Discipline Without Tears* (1972).

It needs to be said right up front that just as there are specific concepts
and skills congruent with an Interventionist school of thought (for example, positive reinforcement, punishment, schedules of reinforcement), so,
too, there are equally, if less well known, specific concepts and skills
congruent with the other two schools of thought. Whatever your philosophy, you will be happier operating in an environment that reflects your
school of thought. After you synthesize your philosophy of how children
learn, grow, and develop, you may want to turn around and question the

questioners—interview the interviewers. Ask them to clarify what their philosophy of education and/or philosophy of discipline is. See if it agrees with yours.

Little New in the Discipline World

One thing that might strike the reader as being odd is the fact that the publication dates for the references listed above (for example, Gordon, Canter, Glasser, Dreikurs, and so on) are all a decade or more old. Why haven't I included newer, more up-to-date, citations? The reason is that there is not a lot new out there on classroom management that is original. For example, Overman's (1979) article on effective student management presents the work of Gordon, Dreikurs, and Glasser. Wolfgang and Glickman's book, *Solving Discipline Problems* (1980), devotes whole chapters to, among just a few others, these same authors.

Four years later, McDaniel's (1984) article once again highlights the same authors. C. M. Charles's book, *Building Classroom Discipline* (1985), lists seven models of discipline including work by Kounin, Glasser, Dreikurs, and Canter. Wolfgang and Glickman's 1986 edition of *Solving Discipline Problems* cites the same authors as their 1980 edition. Finally, the bible of research on teaching, Wittrock's *Handbook of Research on Teaching,* 3d edition (1986, p. 422), cites several comprehensive models related to classroom management—each with its roots in the 1970s, 1960s, or even earlier. They include, in total, "Teacher Effectiveness Training, Transactional Analysis, Assertive Discipline, Reality Therapy, Social Discipline, and Behavior Modification." You would be hard-pressed to pick up an article or book on discipline that did not rehash materials presented elsewhere over the past twenty years. Little new information is being generated on discipline. Let's use this opportunity to catch up on what is known about discipline.

As further evidence that little is new with respect to discipline, one might look at the number of articles published over the years in respected journals having a primary interest in discipline. For instance, the *NASSP Bulletin* is the official publication of the National Association of Secondary School Principals. Its readers, school administrators, certainly have a vested interest in establishing and maintaining classroom, as well as school-wide, discipline. Yet, an examination of their yearly *Index Supplement* for the past decade reveals that less and less is being written, or at least published, on discipline. The number of *NASSP Bulletin* articles indexed under "Discipline" for 1977 through 1981 totals seventy-six. The number indexed for 1982 through 1986 totals just twenty-three.

The plus side of all this is that it is very much worth one's while to learn what is out there on discipline even if the information *appears* to be dated. It is very unlikely that once you spend the energy and time to learn what is currently available on classroom management, that information will become dated. Study it now! Learn it now! Practice it now! I foresee little coming along to take its place that is brand new.

CLASSROOM MANAGEMENT
Hoola Hoops, Pet Rocks, and Rubic's Cubes

As Americans, we seem to find ourselves in a disposable world—diapers, soft drink containers, cigarette lighters, and the latest fads. Hoola hoops, pet rocks, and Rubic's cubes all hit the market, were big (if short-lived) successes, and then disappeared only to be replaced by the next year's fad. This situation is probably okay in the world of business where new products—cars, fashions, toys—are expected each year. Unfortunately that same thinking is not okay when it comes to theories of classroom management. One cannot simply dispose of last year's workable theory of classroom management with the expectation that another new, and equally effective, theory will take its place. It doesn't work that way in education.

There appear to be only a limited number of theories of effective classroom management out there for our use. It makes no sense to dispose of a theory as long as it is working. In fact, I suggest educators hold on for dear life to *any* effective theory of classroom management that works! Don't give up a theory just because its publication date is dated. Don't give up successful theories of classroom management until you know for sure that there is a replacement theory that, when put into practice, is just as, or more, effective.

Playing the Odds

This is what we do in education. We play the odds. Although we could try to use theories that work for all children, at all times, and in all situations, this just does not happen. Instead, we try to use theories that work for *most* children, *most* of the time, in *most* situations. Our goal is to increase the odds that the theories we use will work. "The fact is that in classroom management there are few absolutes, no panaceas, and none who can evidence a 'fail-safe' system" (Hansen 1979, p. 41). This is real life—the life teachers live in.

So it is with theories and techniques of classroom management. No theory or technique works with all children all the time. But there are theories and techniques that work better than others. Let's use these theories for what they can do for us. What about the students upon whom our theories do not work? Well, there will always be these exceptions. What happens, though, is that if you are using theories and techniques that are successful for *most* children *most* of the time in *most* situations, then most students are more often "at task" and, as such, demand less of your time and attention. You can now direct your efforts to either working with the exceptions or identifying and enlisting the aid of others who can offer the help you are ill prepared to offer.

You need to recognize what you CAN do for the child and what you CANNOT do for the child. Be aware of your network of fellow professionals. Use them. Do what you are able to do effectively, and then, if necessary, refer (or seek additional help for) those students you cannot help. This is not a sign of weakness on your part. It is the professional thing to do!

Omission and Commission

The "A" through "Z" suggestions that follow in Chapter II fall into two categories — do's and don'ts. Effective classroom management is influenced just as much by things you do as it is by things you don't do.

The words "you do" and "you don't do" clearly point out that YOU have control over the situation. Teacher behaviors don't occur all by themselves. You can decide to omit certain behaviors that, more often than not, lead to discipline problems. You can also decide to commit certain behaviors that, more often than not, lead to effective discipline. Sins of omission are just as unforgivable in a professional as sins of commission. They are also just as ineffective.

Effective Teaching Must Be Present

Point-blank, no classroom management technique will be effective for very long IF effective teaching is absent. I cannot stress this point strongly enough. Classroom management strategies are NOT substitutes for good teaching. For that matter, good teaching is actually a preventive measure that keeps students so involved and interested that they are not interested in causing discipline problems. For instance, the often-made teacher statement, "When you are able to act in an acceptable manner you will no longer have to stand outside in the hallway," assumes that what is going on in your class is more interesting and exciting than remaining in the hallway. If effective teaching is not taking place in the classroom, then the student will not feel he is missing anything by staying in the hall. Hence, your classroom management statement has no impact.

At the same time, though, this author does not believe that good teaching will prevent all classroom management problems. To that end, even effective teachers must be ready with appropriate strategies of classroom management in order to "keep the learning act afloat." The point is, as in medicine, an "ounce of prevention is worth a pound of cure." If many (certainly not all) discipline problems can be prevented through effective, stimulating, and interesting teaching, then one would be foolish not to take advantage of such teaching. Once again, we are "playing the odds"; trying to use management techniques that work with most children, most of the time, in most situations. Be an effective teacher — first off and foremost.

Is effective teaching all that is needed? No. You must understand that children have much personal history and experience that goes beyond your influence. In the real world, these children cannot simply leave their out-of-school problems at the school's front door in the morning and collect them at day's end. The students' problems will accompany them to your classroom. Skills to manage students, all kinds of students with all kinds of problems, are essential to even the most effective teacher.

Courses in Classroom Management

It is my impression that few teacher education programs have available, and still fewer programs mandate, specific courses in classroom management for their students. I am not alone in holding this view. Hyman and D'Alessandro (1984, p. 42) conclude, "Few U.S. educators have received formal training in the theory, research, and practice of school discipline." McDaniel (1984, p. 71) offers further support when he states:

> Most teachers enter the profession, and persevere in it, with little or no training in school discipline techniques. This is indeed strange when discipline problems are so frequently cited as the greatest dilemma facing public schools. . . . Few states mention behavior management in certification regulations . . . Few colleges or universities require (or even provide) courses in classroom discipline for regular classroom teachers.

The situation is no better for in-service teachers. According to Hansen (1979, p. 41), "A perplexing dilemma for classroom teachers is their uncertain preparation for handling discipline problems." Plax, Kearney, and Tucker (1986, p. 32), citing an earlier comprehensive review of the literature, report that, "beginning elementary and secondary teachers perceive classroom management as their most serious problem." The not-so-surprising effect upon teachers is "that disruptive student behavior is a major factor contributing to teacher stress and job dissatisfaction" (Jones 1984, p. 60).

The situation probably will not get any better in the immediate future given the public's attitude that teachers in training require, if anything, more CONTENT courses, not more PEDAGOGY courses. Today's "blue-ribbon" committees' proposals for strengthening teacher education programs clearly carry the message that teachers need more preparation, but that additional preparation ought not to include more education courses. In fact, many of these reports suggest we already offer too much in the way of education-type courses. If the additional recommendations suggesting that teachers should obtain a liberal arts degree in a content area first AND THEN return for one crash year of teacher training should be implemented, then there will be little room for classroom management courses.

Where then will teachers in training learn classroom management skills? Although it is common for Educational Psychology courses, required of most education majors, to use textbooks that devote at least one chapter to classroom management, this amount of attention probably isn't enough. Perhaps the book you are reading right now can be used as a supplement to your Ed Psych class. Perhaps it can be used as a supplement to other required reading materials in your methods classes. Perhaps it can be kept handy as you plan for your student teaching, and later full-time teaching. Classroom management theories and techniques, in a very readable form, should be kept readily available for repeated reference.

Where Do Teachers Develop Competency in Classroom Management?

Richardson (1985, p. 3) studied teachers' perceptions of their own classroom management behavior. His research shows that teachers attribute that behavior to actual experiences on the job, subsequent years on the job, and student teaching—in that order of importance. Unfortunately, learning while doing seems to be the norm. Course work while in college, what little there is of it, was perceived to be less of a factor in classroom management competency development.

It must be a lonely, as well as threatening, situation for new teachers who must learn classroom management skills on the job. Who can new teachers turn to? Duke (1977) points out that administrators rarely discuss discipline with teachers in specific terms. Supervisors, as well as fellow teachers, were also judged to be of little help.

Although in-service training holds the potential for helping both new and experienced teachers develop classroom management competencies, too often these efforts suffer from "a prevalence of competing approaches, lack of continuing reinforcement, practice and coaching" (Duke and Jones 1984, p. 30).

Read More on Classroom Management

One important part of being a professional is that such a person regularly turns to a recognized body of knowledge in order to solve problems. Chances are, teachers, as professionals, have invested a good deal of their life in acquiring the knowledge and skills that make up that recognized knowledge base. That knowledge base deserves to be regularly used, and, on a continuing basis, updated. People who come to us seeking professional treatment, whether they be students, patients, or clients, deserve, at a minimum, knowledge-based responses.

For instance, I hope medical doctors, as professionals, regularly turn to such a knowledge base—especially when they are treating my illnesses. We all know or have heard of the horrors that can occur when such knowledge is ignored or misapplied. Skyrocketing malpractice insurance is a clear sign that the public will no longer blindly trust health professionals. Surely educators do not think they are immune from similar public challenges. Let's not wait until we, as teachers, have to purchase malpractice insurance. Let's regularly use the appropriate knowledge bases available to us.

Many teachers, and even more of the general public, believe that what teachers do in their profession is nothing more than common sense. This is simply not true. For instance, common sense might tell you that if a student is repeatedly out of his seat, then the teacher should remind him each and every time that he should be sitting down. Yet, assuming the child's motive is to gain attention (see the Chapter III article, "Dreikurs's Goals of Misbehavior"), a far more effective teacher response is to IG-NORE the child's out-of-seat behavior, PRAISE others who are in their seats, and, when it occurs (even out of exhaustion), PRAISE the misbehaving child when he is sitting down. Which teacher response do you believe works best? Only the latter set of responses has a basis in that recognized body of knowledge I keep referring to. Common sense also told us the world was flat, man could not fly, women were only suited for motherhood, and . . . well, you get the message.

Does common sense have a place in education? Sure it does, as long as it has a recognizable foundation in the research literature. It is not uncommon for experienced teachers to dismiss what they do as common sense, when, in fact, it should more correctly be described as "second nature." They have been using a technique for so long that they may have forgotten its origin. Unfortunately, we also have experienced, as well as inexperienced, teachers using techniques that have become second nature to them that *cannot* be supported by the research literature.

A recognized body of knowledge in any field, including education, is really an effort to unravel nature's mysteries and, therefore, should *not* be in conflict with common sense. Nature's truths, once unraveled and understood, should be about as much common sense as they are ever going to get.

Effective disciplinarians are secure in the feeling that they are using techniques that can be defended. All teachers should be prepared to be held accountable — to be ready to explain to any student, parent, fellow teacher, principal, or school board member what they are doing and WHY they are doing what they are doing. The WHY part of this responsibility can only be justified by referring to a recognized body of knowledge.

Make it a regular part of your professional development to read more, more often, on classroom management. Unfortunately, a lot of the quality material written on the topic of discipline does not easily fall into the hands of teachers and other busy practitioners. For instance, *The Seventy-Eighth Yearbook of the National Society for the Study of Education* (Duke 1978) is entirely devoted to classroom management. Most teachers will never get (or take) the opportunity to read it.

The same goes for the *Handbook of Research on Teaching*, 3d edition (Wittrock 1986). Although this thousand-page resource (in particular, Chapter 3, "Classroom Organization and Management" [Doyle]) offers thirty-two pages of research on classroom management, complete with 300 references, few students in teacher training, and even fewer teachers, will ever lay their hands on it. This is not intended to be a "put-down" to students in teacher training or to busy teachers. It is just a fact. Teachers, especially, need more readable and more readily available information on classroom management.

Chapter II of this book, with its "A" through "Z" suggestions, will help you establish and maintain better classroom discipline. But Chapter II, by design, limits your exposure to theory. Chapter III, with its longer articles, presents classroom management ideas backed up by a little more theory. Chapter IV, on ERIC, describes a system for getting still more information on discipline — anything from practice to theory.

Just as you might remind your students that learning is a lifelong endeavor, I remind you that classroom management is not simply something that can be totally presented between the covers of a book — even this one. What is presented in this book will certainly get you started in the right direction. But, like any single book or article, it is not enough. Read more, more often, on classroom management. Make it a habit.

Doctor, Doctor, I Have This Pain!

We are probably all familiar with the temptation to get some free advice from medical doctors if we happen to run into them at a party. Come to think of it, I catch myself trying to get free advice from lawyers, accountants, brick layers, septic tank installers, and airline employees when I see them at informal gatherings. It is no different for authors of books on classroom management.

Most readers probably have a specific child in mind about whom they would like to ask. Their question would start out, "I have this second grader who does such and such. What should I do with him?" Well, given that this is a book, you can't directly ask me that question, and I can't directly give you an answer. Instead, I ask that you keep that child in mind as you read what follows. Continually ask yourself, "How could I use one or more of the "A" through "Z" suggestions?" or "How could I apply what is presented in the slightly longer articles in Chapter III?" or "How could I use ERIC, the information retrieval system described in Chapter IV, to get more help in dealing with this child?"

Read this book with a purpose. Continually ask yourself how *you* could apply this material with *your* children in *your* unique set of circumstances. Do it; it works!

Classroom Mangement Skills Are Crucial

Charles (1981, p. 13), best supports this heading by saying:

> Discipline, class control, classroom management — by whatever name you call it, keeping order in the classroom is a teacher's greatest concern. You may not like that fact; you may wish it weren't true. But it is. That's a given in the daily life of teachers.

> Discipline is so crucial, so basic to everything else in the classroom, that most educators agree: it is the one thing that makes or breaks teachers. . . . It needn't be the whole class that misbehaves. Three or four students, even one, can so disrupt a class that learning becomes impossible for even the best behaved students.

Read this book with the aim of putting into practice the "A" through "Z" suggestions. Work on making them part of your repertoire of classroom management behaviors. Tackle them a few at a time. Select those suggestions that can be put into practice immediately, and do so. Gradually incorporate the remaining suggestions.

Read the slightly longer articles in Chapter III, and consider how they can enhance your basis of classroom management. Tackle them one at a time. Finally, identify those areas where you believe you still need more information and skills. Turn to Chapter IV, and use ERIC to locate and to access what you need. You will not be disappointed.

Get started!

REFERENCES

Axelrod, S. (1977). *Behavior modification for the classroom teacher.* New York: McGraw-Hill.

Canter, C., & Canter, M. (1976). *Assertive discipline.* Seal Beach, CA: Canter and Associates.

Charles, C. (1981). *Building classroom discipline.* New York: Longman.

Dobson, J. (1970). *Dare to discipline.* Wheaton, IL: Tyndale House.

Doyle, W. (1986). Classroom organization and management. In M. Wittrock (Ed.), Handbook of research and teaching (Chap. 14). New York: Macmillan Publishing Company.

Dreikurs, R., & Cassel, P. (1972). *Discipline without tears.* New York: Hawthorne.

Duke, D. (1977). A systematic management plan for school discipline. *NASSP Bulletin, 61*(405), 1–10. EJ 158-808.

Duke, D. (ed.) (1979). *Classroom management. The Seventy-eighth Yearbook of the National Society for the Study of Education.* Chicago: The University of Chicago Press.

Duke, D., & Jones, V. (1984). Two decades of discipline—Assessing the development of an educational specialization. *Journal of Research and Development in Education, 17*(4), 25–35. EJ 302-053.

Elam, S. (1989). The second Gallup/Phi Delta Kappa poll of teachers' attitudes toward the public schools. *Phi Delta Kappan, 70*(10), 785–798. No EJ number yet assigned.

Glasser, W. (1969). *Schools without failure.* New York: Harper & Row.

Gordon, T. (1970). *Parent effectiveness training.* New York: Peter H. Wyden.

Gordon, T. (1974). *Teacher effectiveness training.* New York: David McKay Co.

Hansen, J. (1979). Discipline and classroom management: Different strokes for different folks. *NASSP Bulletin, 63*(428), 40–47. EJ 206-325.

Hyman, I., & D'Alessandro, J. (1984). Good, old-fashioned discipline: The politics of punitiveness. *Phi Delta Kappan, 66*(1), 39–45. EJ 306-689.

Jones, V. (1984). An administrator's guide to developing and evaluating a building discipline program. *NASSP Bulletin, 68*(471), 60–73. EJ 298-007.

McDaniel, T. (1984). Developing the skills of humanistic discipline. *Educational Leadership, 41*(8), 71–74. EJ 299-545.

Overman, W. (1979). Effective communication: The key to student management. *NASSP Bulletin, 63*(428), 34–39. EJ 206-324.

Plax, T., Kearney, P., & Tucker, L. (1986). Prospective teachers' use of behavior alteration techniques on common student misbehaviors. *Communication Education, 35*(1), 32–41. EJ 331-073.

Richardson, M. (1985). Perceptions of principals and teachers of effective management of student behavior. *SPECTRUM, 3*(3), 25–30. EJ 325-249.

Rogers, C. (1969). *Freedom to learn.* Columbus, OH: Merrill.

Wittrock, M. (Ed.). (1986). *Handbook of research on teaching,* 3d edition. New York: Macmillan Publishing Company.

Wolfgang, C., & Glickman, C. (1980). *Solving discipline problems.* Boston: Allyn and Bacon, Inc.

Wolfgang, C., & Glickman, C. (1986). *Solving discipline problems.* Boston: Allyn and Bacon, Inc.

Note: The EJ number (for example, EJ 306-689) that follows each journal article can be used, in conjunction with the ERIC system described in Chapter IV, to obtain a copy of that article.

"A" Through "Z" Suggestions

Discipline problems do not just occur out of the blue, they are precipitated. Home and other outside-of-school environments exert a major influence upon children which, in turn, affects their readiness to learn when they come to school. As teachers, we can't do a whole lot about these outside-of-school factors. We can, though, address those in-school factors that influence a child's willingness to learn. The following "A" through "Z" suggestions, when regularly and consciously applied, will improve classroom management.

Will you find anything new in the suggestions that follow? Shrigley (1985, p. 31) provides an answer to that question when he states: "I concede that successful teachers have been using many of the coping skills casually; however, I challenge them to consciously sequence the coping skills into a systematic plan."

Successful teachers may respond to many of the following suggestions by saying, "We already do it." While that may be true for them, most student teachers and new teachers can't respond with such confidence.

For those who might think that they are teachers, not disciplinarians, I offer the following: In the real world of the classroom, one cannot choose to be one and avoid being the other. Discipline is a prerequisite to successful teaching. Effective classroom management is only a *means* to an *end*—effective teaching and effective learning. Discipline is a necessary, *but not sufficient,* condition for effective teaching.

All of the "A" through "Z" suggestions that follow are things you can do on your own. None involves any major change in school or departmental policy. Are these suggestions simply tricks of the trade? Not really. Each suggestion has a grounding in theory. Take advantage of these suggestions. Use these suggestions. Get started now!

Those readers who are looking for a single theoretical thread to connect each of the alphabetized suggestions may be disappointed at first. Classroom management books are of two forms: the type that takes the eclectic approach, and the kind that promotes a specialized system. This book is, and was intended to be, an example of the eclectic approach. Chapter II, as reviewed by teacher educators and basic education practitioners, is seen as loaded with proven ideas and techniques to enhance good classroom discipline.

Although there is no single, overall organizing scheme to Chapter II beyond the ABC format, many of the suggestions can logically be grouped or categorized. Some of these categories are shown below. You are encouraged to create still other categories *and* to continue adding to your repertoire of classroom management strategies.

Suggestions: Respect for Students

C for **C**aring for Students *and* Showing It
C for Individual or Private **C**orrection
H for Seal It with a **H**andshake
L for **L**isten to Your Students
M for **M**r. or **M**iss
N for Learn Their **N**ames
T for Say "**T**hank You"

Suggestions: Preventing Discipline Problems

G for Make School a **G**ood Place to Be
K for **K**ounin's Withitness
L for **L**egitimization: Where to Place the Sidewalks?
O for **O**rganized and **O**verlapping
O for **O**ver-prepare
R for **R**ules and Procedures

Suggestions: Behavioral Modification Techniques

C for **C**atch Students Being Good
C for **C**onsequences (Logical, Natural, *and* Contrived)
E for **E**xtinguish Unwanted Behaviors
E for Modify **E**nvironment
I for **I**gnore Inappropriate Behavior
P for **P**remack Principle or Grandma's Rule
P for **P**unishment; In Practice Who Really Supports It?
Q for **Q**ualifier for Punishment

Suggestions: Alternative Ways to Respond to Student Problems

I for Send **I**-Messages, Not You-Messages
Y for Don't Ask **Why**
Z for **Z**ap Solution Messages

Suggestions: Conveying a Professional Attitude

C for **C**alm and Businesslike
C for Use Your **C**olleagues
G for Don't Hold a **G**rudge
U for Be **U**p
P for Don't Take It **P**ersonally
X for **Ex**emplify Desired Behavior; Don't Be a Hypocrite

Suggestions: Specific Classroom-Related Techniques

A for **A**ct, Don't Just React
A for **A**ssign Responsibility
B for **B**ack Away
E for **E**ncourage vs. Praise

E for **E**ye Messages
P for **P**unctuality
R for **R**eturn Assignments and Tests Quickly
S for **S**ecure Their Attention—First!
T for **T**eams; An Important Aspect of Control Theory
V for **V**isibility (and at Times Invisibility)
W for **W**ait-Time
W for Use **We**, Not You

Suggestions: Keeping a Teacher's Role in Perspective

F for **F**riendly vs. **F**riends
J for **J**udge and **J**ury
L for **L**egitimate Power, Don't Abuse It
T for **T**hreats and Warnings

Suggestions: Just in Case

D for Make a **D**eal with a Fellow Teacher
E for Prepare an **E**mergency Plan

Suggestions: Knowing Your Students

D for Student **D**iversity
S for **S**urprise Them or "How Did You Know That?"
V for **V**ocational Technical School Experience

Is the ABC format in Chapter II a little corny? Perhaps. Yet, the ABC format was never intended to be anything more than it is—a way to highlight a series of straightforward and practical classroom management suggestions. One reviewer described the ABC format as catchy and a change from the dry, sterile publications one sees so often now. The suggestions in Chapter II are designed to be down-to-earth, clear and understandable, and relatively short and to the point.

The listing below represents the "A" through "Z" suggestions.

A for **A**ct, Don't Just React

There is a big difference between acting and reacting. To act is to be in command; to react is to have the situation be in command. Teachers should do more acting—taking charge using the best knowledge base available—and less reacting, letting the circumstances dictate their behavior. Teachers who spend their time reacting are always followers— waiting until something happens before they take action. Teachers who spend their time acting are leaders—more often controlling what happens, whether in classroom instruction or in classroom management.

Don't be a "fire putter outer." This is someone who, in effect, looks at classroom management as a tool similar to a fire extinguisher. In the fire extinguisher analogy, classroom management techniques are kept handy for WHEN, and IF, discipline problems occur, so that they can be used to douse the discipline fire. In reality, the question is not IF discipline problems occur, but WHEN discipline problems occur. Whereas most people hope they will never have to use the available fire extinguisher, that is an unrealistic expectation with regards to classroom management strategies.

Teachers should spend time prior to the start of school planning their discipline strategies just as they spend time planning teaching strategies and ordering teaching materials. Discipline must be established, and discipline must be maintained throughout the school year. Skills are needed to make it happen.

I suppose the teaching profession is not too unlike the medical profession, where we give lip service to preventive measures, yet still wait too often for symptoms to show before we take action. The "ounce of prevention is worth a pound of cure" adage applies as much in education as it does in medicine. Making things happen by acting is much preferred to letting things happen by simply reacting. Effective teachers act, they don't simply react!

A for Assign Responsibility

The more responsible students are for their own behaviors, the less need there will be for teacher-supplied classroom management. Therefore, if for no other reason than to reduce the time and energy devoted to classroom management, teachers should work to increase the pool of responsible students.

Too often teachers assign responsibility only to those students who have already shown they are responsible. What point is there to curing the already cured? How do students who are not responsible ever learn to become more responsible unless they are given practice with being responsible? It reminds me of a childhood friend whose mother said he was allowed to go swimming with us only after he learned how to swim! He never did go swimming with us. To this day he still cannot swim.

Learning to be more responsible is much like learning anything else. It involves a process of trial and error—hopefully more of the former than of the latter. Yet, teachers often treat learning responsibility as something completely different from other learning.

For instance, if a student were just starting to learn trigonometry, a teacher would require that the student practice solving trig problems (trial component). At the same time, the teacher would expect the student to make some mistakes, to occasionally fail, and even periodically to regress (error component). But, "some mistakes" and "occasionally fail" would not be enough evidence to assume that the student was incapable of doing trigonometry. So too, when students occasionally fall short of being as responsible as we might have hoped, it would be equally unfair to assume they are incapable of being responsible.

Assigning responsibility can take many forms. A teacher could assign less responsible students the in-class tasks of distributing materials, helping to collect assignments, and so on. Later, the teacher could use out-of-class, yet well-defined and controlled, activities such as having a student take attendance forms to the office. Another example might be a teacher's assigning an older student the responsibility of working with a younger student—perhaps teaching her a specific academic skill or showing him how to use a piece of playground equipment.

The general rule would be that the assigned tasks would start off small and build in importance and trust as the student showed he or she was capable of handling responsibility.

Just as it is true that "nothing breeds success like success," "nothing breeds responsibility like responsibility." Although increasing student responsibility is, in and of itself, a desirable goal, remember its implication in the area of classroom and school discipline. More responsible students require less external (teacher-supplied) discipline.

B for Back Away

When you call upon a student to answer a question or acknowledge a student who has asked a question, the "natural" tendency is to move closer to him. When you do this, what happens? The closer you move in his direction the quieter his answer or question will be. After all, why should he speak loudly when you are, or soon will be, right next to him? What ends up happening is that the two of you carry on a dialogue and the rest of the class feels left out.

What else happens as you approach the student who is speaking? Your line of sight, your eye contact, with the rest of the class is lost. When your eye contact is lost, your nonverbal communication with the class is lost, too.

If other students cannot hear what that one student is saying, if they  lose eye contact with you, and if, as a result, they no longer feel involved in the discussion, their attention will turn elsewhere. Often this "elsewhere" results in the need for the teacher to take disciplinary measures. It doesn't have to happen.

Keep your students involved in what is happening in class discussions. When calling upon a student to answer, BACK AWAY from him. This forces him to increase the volume of his voice so that you can hear him from across the room. If you can hear him, so can all of the other students!

Moving away from the student who is answering leaves you with a clear line of sight across the entire class. You can see the student who is answering. But, you can see the faces of many of the other students—perhaps one or more of whom have "approving" or "disapproving" looks on their faces and can then be asked to comment. The student with the "confused" look can be straightened out. The students over in the corner just beginning a little neighborly conversation can be thwarted. The discussion continues; all are involved.

As effective as the BACK AWAY concept is, occasionally do the exact opposite. Move very close to the person who is answering—eye to eye. Put the student on the spot. Invade his personal space—but not for too long —just long enough so that students do not know what to expect. In football it would be like having a strong running game, but every once in a while going to the air with a pass. The other side never knows what play might come next. The quarterback who varies his game plan is usually more effective in the long run—so, too, with teachers.

Do move about the classroom. Look at your notes ahead of time, and judge which portions of the lecture you can deliver while away from the desk or podium. Consider using an overhead projector that has a brief outline of your notes on it. This would free you to move about the room and more closely monitor student behavior. Let a student seated by the overhead uncover sections at a time, so you don't have to run to the front of the room. A flip chart with the same brief outline might work as well to free you from teaching solely in the front of the room.

Your movement about the classroom takes advantage of another well-known classroom management tool—proximity control. The closer you are to students the more likely they are to remain at task, and, consequently, the less likely they are to misbehave.

C for Calm and Businesslike

When disciplining a student, do so calmly. I cannot stress this point strongly enough! Save your emotional energy for more appropriate times—animated lectures, spirited class discussions. Be businesslike, polite but firm, as you go about disciplining a student. Even a misbehaving child is entitled to respect. A police officer that pulls you over for speeding has every right to implement the State's discipline plan—write you a ticket. He has no right to belittle you, to rant and rave at you.

When a student misbehaves, get on with the act of implementing your discipline plan. Skip the screaming, finger shaking, penetrating looks, sarcastic comments, and so on. Implementing your discipline plan in a calm manner keeps the misbehaving student's attention on the relationship between his behavior and the logical consequences that flow from that behavior. The ongoing relationship the two of you have is far less likely to be weakened. Remember, although the discipline episode will pass, you and the student must work together for the rest of the year.

I know of no author writing on the subject of discipline, nor of any theory of discipline, who would condone any other teacher posture than remaining calm and businesslike when disciplining a student. If you let students "set you off," "*make* you lose your temper," then you are no longer in control! Whether it is a petite 105-pound female or a 210-pound male, the thought of the only "adult" in the classroom being out of control is very scary. You are the teacher, you are supposed to be in control. To control others effectively, you must first control yourself!

One other important reason for remaining calm and businesslike when you discipline students is that your behavior will be a model for them. Discipline yourself in manners, voice, disposition, honesty, punctuality, consistency, fairness, and so on (Stefanich and Bell 1985, p. 20). Students will learn not only from the specific discipline you dispense, but also from *how* you dispense it. When you lose control, your unintended lesson, one of "flying off the handle," could well be remembered longer than the intended discipline lesson.

Be conscious of how you act when you discipline students. Others surely are—I guarantee it! Work at being able to discipline a student with as little disturbance to the normal classroom operation as possible. Teacher calmness has another thing going for it; students prefer it. Students judge as one characteristic of their "best" teachers that such teachers remain calm when telling off miscreants (Lewis and Lovegrove 1984).

Everything is to be gained by disciplining in a calm and businesslike manner. *Nothing* is to be gained by doing otherwise.

C for Caring for Students *and* Showing It

Does this point really need to be made? Yes and no. Surely, an overwhelming number of teachers believe that they care about their students. Why else would they have become teachers? On the other hand, caring for students must be conveyed, not just felt, in order to be effective in positively influencing students' behavior.

How many human relationships in other arenas such as a marriage have suffered because, although the feelings may have been present (for example, love, caring, respect), little conscious effort was made to convey these feelings in a way that could be seen? Is it that we are somehow supposed to sense that others feel the way they do? Perhaps, but it certainly would do little harm to show our feelings in as tangible a way as possible. Send those roses, make that special phone call, prepare that special dish.

So, too, it is in education. Palonsky (1977) reports that teachers' interpersonal skills are more important than their instructional skills in classroom management. One interpersonal skill, caring, and the degree to which it is perceived to exist are identified as the primary elements for controlling behavior problems.

How might teachers show that they care? Giving students the "time of day" as they come into school or into the classroom is a good start. In addition, a teacher could show he or she cares by regularly using other Chapter II suggestions listed in this book including, among others, Catch Children Being Good; Send *I*-Messages, Not You-Messages; Learn Their Names; Listen to Your Students; Surprise Them or "How Did You Know That?"; and Say "Thank You."

A school where teachers care, and show that they care, is perceived by students to be a "good place." It is a place where students want to be. It is filled with people whom students want to be around. When school is perceived as a good place, the stage is set for, (1) fewer discipline problems to occur in the first place, and (2) strategies of classroom management to be more successful when used. Note the prerequisite of school's being perceived by students as a good place in order to use Glasser's Reality Therapy. See the Chapter III article, "Glasser's Reality Therapy."

Everyone agrees that "an ounce of prevention is worth a pound of cure." To that end, Hyman and D'Alessandro (1984, p. 43) report that, "Caring . . . teachers go a long way toward preventing serious discipline problems from arising in the first place."

C for Catch Students Being Good

This suggestion deals with teachers trying to catch students being good, not just catching them being bad. Given that students' behavior in the future is, to a great degree, governed by the consequences of their present behavior, it makes just as much sense to reward good behavior as it does to punish bad behavior. In fact, it makes more sense.

Make sure students know they have been caught! Try sending an appreciative I-Message to those students whom you catch being good. You might say, "Class, when all of you are sitting at your seats so quietly doing your work, it makes it possible for me to help other students who need assistance, and I really appreciate it." Or, you could say, "Class, when you put your materials away after our art time, it saves me a lot of time and effort, and I really want to thank you." Finally, you could say, "When all of you continue doing your seat work when I am called out in the hall to talk to the principal, it helps convey to the principal that I am doing a good job as a teacher. That makes me feel proud. Thanks!"

In each of these examples, I assume that the teacher actually feels the way she says she feels. Why not simply acknowledge these feelings and supporting facts? Catch the students being good *and* LET THEM KNOW THAT YOU HAVE CAUGHT THEM! See the Chapter II suggestion Send *I*-Messages, Not You-Messages, and the Chapter III article, "Gordon's Teacher (Parent) Effectiveness Training," for more information on I-Messages.

Sometimes catching students being good, as an effort to enhance students' acceptable behaviors, can also be used to lessen unacceptable behaviors. This is done by trying to catch students engaging in behavior that is *incompatible* with the behavior the teacher is trying to stop. For instance, the behavior of a student sitting in his seat doing his work is incompatible with the behavior of that same student's being out of his seat wandering about the classroom. A student cannot do both at the same time—the two behaviors are incompatible. If the teacher's goal is to reduce the student's out-of-seat behavior, a traditional response might be to punish the student for being out of his seat. A more effective way to accomplish this same goal is for the teacher to catch the student in his seat and provide a desired consequence.

The more that students are "caught" being good, the more reason they have to continue being good. The more that students are "caught" being good, the less reason they have to misbehave.

C for Use Your Colleagues

Books on classroom management are great resources—especially, of course, this book. They are readily available, relatively inexpensive, and permit you to set your own learning pace. They are there as a reference now or in the future. But books alone are not the only great resources available to teachers seeking knowledge and skills relating to strategies of classroom management.

A nationwide information and retrieval system, readily accessible to practitioners, such as the one described in Chapter IV, Educational Resources Information Center (ERIC), is a dream come true. In-service workshops, courses, and workshops abound. A lot is out there to help teachers with what it takes to establish and maintain good classroom discipline.

But, one does not have to always look "out there." Why not look down the hall or perhaps to the classroom next door? What I am getting at is for you to take advantage of some of the best resources available anywhere—your fellow teachers—your colleagues. Collectively, your school probably has a staff with decades upon decades of experience. Many teachers have not only the very definite advantage of knowing their material, but also of knowing their community, their children, and their children's parents. This is an advantage that many textbooks, seminars, and highly paid consultants lack.

Try these two strategies. With perhaps the recommendation of your principal or department head, ask to observe fellow teachers as they teach. But go into your observation with a focus. This time it may be classroom management strategies, next time it may be how to manage small group projects, and so on. In any case, make it a point to identify specific techniques that seem to work. Start yourself a notebook of successful ideas. If possible, meet with the teacher before and after the observation. Determine what she is setting out to accomplish. After the observation, discuss what you observed. Ask questions, seek clarification.

Next, ask selected teachers to come in and observe your classes. Provide your observer with a focus—classroom management, in our case. Fellow teachers are a bit less threatening than a principal or supervisor. Fellow teachers are closer to your world of reality—they just left one class, and they are just about to go to another. The observation of your class is probably sandwiched in between.

Do these two activities early in the year. Ask to observe fellow teachers' classes, *and* ask that they observe your classes BEFORE discipline becomes a problem. What you will learn from observing their classes and what they might have to say about your classes will be far more beneficial if learned early.

Where will fellow teachers find the time and the energy to observe your classes? Take my word for it, they will make time. Most seasoned teachers find it flattering when a younger teacher asks for guidance.

Erik Erikson (1963), in his eight stages of psychosocial development, offers a rationale as to why seasoned teachers would so willingly respond to your requests. By helping you, they are helping themselves to negotiate successfully their Generativity vs. Self-Absorption life crisis—a normal part of middle adulthood. According to Erikson, middle-aged people "acquire a genuine concern for the welfare of future generations which results in providing unselfish guidance to younger people" (Weiten 1989, p. 413).

C for Consequences (Logical, Natural, *and* Contrived)

There is no doubt that people's future behavior is influenced by the consequences of their present, as well as past, behavior. Some would even say consequences *control* people's future behavior. Whether it is control or influence, consequences do make a difference. If we receive pleasant consequences following our behavior, we are more inclined to engage in those same behaviors more often and more intensely in the future. On the other hand, if we receive unpleasant consequences, we are less inclined to engage in those behaviors in the future. But, what consequences are we talking about?

If we were to list examples of specific consequences that could be provided to learners, the list would be endless—thus of little use to educators. If, instead, we were to group these specific consequences by categories, we would find that there are only three: natural, logical, and contrived consequences.

Natural consequences are those that "naturally" flow from someone's behaviors. They are not imposed by anyone else—teacher, parent, spouse, boss. If anyone is responsible for supplying natural consequences, it is nature itself. If a child has body odor, nature has designed it so that others will sense (smell) the odor and naturally avoid the child's company. No adult had to tell the other children to engage in avoidance behavior. If a student does not study for a test, then, naturally, the odds are that he will do less well than if he had studied. Nature, and the fact that nature has designed a relationship between studying and performance, supplies the unpleasant consequence—doing less well on the test. Adults who drive too fast for icy weather conditions are more likely to skid off the road. Nature, and its relationship between "tire adhesion" and "weather conditions," may very well supply the unpleasant consequence of an accident.

Logical consequences are those supplied by someone else, not by nature. To a reasoning person, supplying logical consequences makes sense. There is a recognizable connection between a student's behavior and the consequence supplied by a teacher. If a child has body odor, it would be logical (reasonable) for a principal to require that the child attend to personal hygiene before being permitted to return to class. If a student does not study for a test and does poorly, it would be logical for a teacher to require that the student continue studying the material and take a makeup test before being permitted to go on. For the adult who drove too fast and experienced the automobile accident, it would be logical for the insurance company to raise his premiums.

Contrived consequences are invented or fabricated by someone else. But, unlike logical consequences, a reasoning person would have difficulty understanding the connection between the misbehavior and the supplied consequence. With contrived consequences, it is not at all clear why a supplied consequence follows from one's behavior. No logical connection exists. If a child has body odor, a contrived consequence would be to have him write 500 times, "I will always come to school clean." If a student does poorly on a test, a contrived consequence would be to have him do a hundred laps around the gym. For the adult who had the automobile accident, a contrived consequence would be to have him do seventy-five hours of public service work in the park. It is almost as if the consequence supplier pulled the consequence out of midair.

What might be a synonym for contrived consequences—supplied consequences that do not logically or naturally flow from a student's misbehaviors? If you guessed "punishment," then you are correct. Contrived consequences are most often just another way of saying punishment.

Where possible, structure the environment so that natural consequences will likely occur. They are the best teachers. They accompany each of us out in the real world. Body odor will cause us to lose friends. Chances are we will take corrective measures. Not studying for tests will cause lower performance. Chances are, next time we will adjust our studying habits. Driving too fast will cause accidents. Chances are, we will be more careful in the future. Not wearing proper winter clothes will usually result in illness. Chances are, we will take corrective measures.

When natural consequences are not likely to occur, try your very best to supply logical consequences. They work next best. They work because students can see that the consequence you are supplying is somehow connected to their behavior. It is predictable; it makes sense. It may even be judged as "fair." This is not to say that students graciously accept logical consequences; they don't always. But, logical consequences depend less upon the whim or capriciousness of the consequence supplier. They are more impersonal. A student's behavior, something he has control over, triggers a supplied consequence. If the offender changes his behavior, he can change the supplied consequences. It is entirely in the hands of the misbehaving student. This sets the stage for students to take responsibility for their own behaviors.

Educators normally have a difficult time justifying the supplying of contrived consequences. Natural or logical connections are lacking between the misbehavior and the supplied consequences. Contrived consequences are taken "personally." This undermines their effectiveness. Avoid contrived consequences at all costs. Use the more effective alternatives—natural and logical consequences!

C for Individual or Private Correction

Correction is an integral part of classroom discipline. How one corrects students can make the difference between achieving effective and ineffective results. More effective results are achieved when teachers individually and privately correct students.

According to Lasley (1981, p. 9), "Individualized corrections are directed only at those students who exhibit misbehavior. Direct, individual commands are difficult for students to ignore." Saying, "David, put your library book away, and start your math exercises on page ten," or issuing the command, "Becky, stop passing notes, and get your assignments ready to take home," makes it clear to whom the teacher is talking and what the teacher expects David and Becky to do. Generalized comments like, "Everyone get busy," might enable David to keep reading his library book and Becky to continue passing notes while at the same time assuming they are, in fact, "busy."

Private correction is generally unobtrusive to classroom processes and audible to almost no one other than the misbehaving student, or at least to only a small group of nearby pupils. Only the teacher and the misbehaving student are involved. Because no one else is involved, neither the teacher nor the student is under quite so much pressure to take a stand and save face by not backing down (Lasley 1981). Private correction follows the adage, "Praise in public (except perhaps some secondary students), punish in private."

Shrigley (1985, pp. 26–27) presents four intervention skills, a form of teacher telegraphy, designed to privately inform disruptive students that their behavior is unacceptable. These skills, in hierarchical order are: ignore the behavior, signals, proximity control, and touch control. Teachers may choose to use "planned ignoring," if only briefly, for slight infractions. Inaudible facial expressions and gestures, such as putting your index finger up to your lips, serve to put the misbehaving student on notice. Proximity control, or standing near the misbehaving student, is the next step. Finally, subtle and unobtrusive touch control (with appropriate age and gender considerations) leaves little doubt in the student's mind that you disapprove of his or her behavior.

If you are going to correct student misbehavior, do it effectively. Provide individual correction and private correction.

D for Make a Deal with a Fellow Teacher

To use operant conditioning principles effectively, one must be aware of the four available teacher-supplied consequences. These include positive reinforcement, negative reinforcement (see the Chapter III article, "Negative Reinforcement"), time-out, and punishment. This suggestion deals with time-out as a teacher-supplied consequence.

Consider striking a deal with a fellow teacher, often one who is teaching students of a different grade level than yours, where he will take your "problem child" and you will take his. In an elementary school, your sixth grade problem, John, could be sent temporarily to Miss Logan's second grade classroom. Miss Logan is primed to expect occasionally a sixth grade "guest." She knows that he has been sent to her as sort of a time-out arrangement. She knows that he has work to do and is to get on with it. No fuss, no bother.

This is a less drastic and less punitive, as well as more pedagogically sound, classroom management technique than putting him out in the hall or sending him to the office. The technique removes John from an environment in which, at least for the present, he is having trouble coping. Going to Miss Logan's room temporarily removes John from his friends, his peers, his audience. In turn, Miss Logan may occasionally send one of her second graders to your sixth grade classroom.

Note, the purpose of striking a deal with a fellow teacher is *not* to embarrass or punish the child—that is a whole separate operant learning consequence called punishment. The purpose is simply to place the child in a different environment where he can once again get back at task. There should be no particular fanfare and no fuss made when the student is moved from one room to another. It should be done as smoothly and congenially as possible. There should be no finger shaking, tongue lashing, calling the sixth grader a "little second grader," and so on. Time-out as a classroom management technique is not punishment. Do not, by your inappropriate execution of a time-out arrangement, accidentally turn time-out into punishment!

How long is his temporary stay in Miss Logan's room? That depends. It could be YOUR DECISION when you think he is ready to return and join his fellow sixth graders. It could be HIS DECISION, if you so agree, to return when he thinks he is capable of returning.

More and more high schools have instituted In School Suspensions

(ISS) programs. Perhaps before this drastic step is taken, a "Let's Make a Deal" arrangement with a fellow teacher should be tried.

D for Student Diversity

"Wow! I do have a rather diverse group of children in my class, don't I?" This could be the revelation of many of today's new teachers when they student teach or secure that first full-time teaching job.

Students come in colors—black, white, brown, yellow, and red. For teachers who come from middle- to lower-middle-class white backgrounds, and most do, this is a real eye-opener. Is it "okay" to call black kids "colored"? What about calling them "Negroes"? Technically, who qualifies as Southeast Asian, and who does not? What is the proper term, "Hispanics" or "Mexican-Americans"? Whom do I place in the "Other" category on my attendance register? What color are "Other" people?

Students come to school with various religious beliefs—some with no beliefs at all. What do I do about that test I have scheduled for the same day as Rosh Hashanah—a Jewish holy day? If I schedule a Christmas gift exchange party will I offend non-Christians? If I don't have some sort of Christmas party will I offend Christians? Will some students refuse to take part in a pro/con discussion of abortion, birth control, evolution? What will I do if a student refuses? Will this warrant disciplinary measures?

More and more of our students will come from single-parent homes. Statistics show that forty percent of the children today will be living with a single parent by their eighteenth birthday (National Education Association 1987, p. 23). Most of these children will lack an appropriate male role model in their lives. Do I catch myself falling into the trap of thinking, "Well, what can you expect from Johnny? There is no father present to discipline him."

Single parents, most often women, will typically have incomes near or below the poverty level. What impact will that have upon projects and other outside-of-class activities I assign? The cost of project materials may well equal the cost of a gallon of milk, a pound of bologna, and a loaf of bread. Will such an assignment penalize less affluent children so that their self-esteem is lowered? Will they strike back? Will I discipline them when they do?

Whether children come from single-parent families or from dual-parent families, more and more students today are "latchkey" children—carrying their front door key on a string around their neck because neither working-mom nor working-dad are there to greet them when they get home from school. The National Education Association estimates that thirty percent of today's students are latchkey children (1987, p. 23). Do I call a misbehaving student's parents at work? When will David's parents be able to come in to talk about his misbehavior? Is it reasonable to expect them to take off from work? Should I set up a meeting in the evening?

Students come in all ability levels—some mentally gifted, some mentally handicapped; some TMR, EMR, or LD; some normal (whatever that is). Students come with physical handicaps. Nationwide efforts to mainstream special children as a result of Public Law 94-142, passed by the Congress in 1975, have changed the makeup of many of today's classrooms. It has also changed the demands upon a teacher's time, talent, and energy. The time and effort required to write IEPs (Individual Education Programs) for handicapped children, as well as to carry out these IEPs, was never envisioned in teachers' minds just two decades ago.

Some students have undetected hearing and sight problems. Could it be that Heather, who is forever asking me to repeat instructions, IS paying attention but she just cannot hear me? Have I responded by disciplining her? Could it be that Barry, who always seems to be leaning across the aisle copying Wendy's work, simply cannot see the board? Have I treated this as "breaking the rules" and punished him accordingly?

Some students come to school who do not, as Glasser (1986, p. 38) describes it, "have learning pictures in their heads to work in school." "What students (and all of us) do in school (and out) is completely determined by the pictures in their heads" (Glasser 1986, p. 39). What would you do if you were compelled to spend day after day in an environment where you did not picture yourself as possibly succeeding? Causing problems would be an attractive way to strike back.

Some students—as many as fifteen percent (National Education Association 1987, p. 23)—do not speak English. Is it unreasonable to expect their parents to read to them? to check their homework? to help them with their homework? Without this home support, are some students more likely to have academic problems that could then spill over into discipline problems? What are you going to do about it?

Some students come from homes where education is not highly valued. Many parents, even those who could afford to do so, do not take a daily newspaper nor do they subscribe to monthly magazines. Testimonies of educational achievements, such as graduation pictures, do not adorn their fireplace mantels. Appropriate study areas are not available. Many children (and parents) from such homes either do not have a library card, or if they do, make little use of it.

So, your students may not be just like you, their teacher. So what? You are there as their teacher, so get on with your teaching. Be knowledgeable of your students' diverse backgrounds. Be sensitive to these individual and cultural differences. But keep your standards high— realistic, but high. The worst thing you could do is to use your students' diversity as an excuse for expecting less from them than what they are capable of achieving. Realistic, but high, expectations will challenge them without overwhelming them. This approach—this attitude—produces greater learning and, as a result, fewer discipline problems.

E for Prepare an Emergency Plan

Prepare a plan to handle those school or classroom emergencies (health, discipline, and so on) that may occur in a teacher's life. It should go without saying that the time to form an emergency plan is *not* during an actual emergency. The plan should be worked out ahead of time.

For instance, a teacher may need to take a child who has suddenly become ill to the nurse. What is the teacher to do with the rest of the class? Simply telling them to keep on with their work may not be the best answer. A teacher could work out, ahead of time, a code that when quickly delivered to a fellow teacher would tell that teacher to "please keep an eye on my unsupervised class while I attend to an emergency." No long explanation would be required—the code word would simply and quickly execute the emergency plan.

Have you ever been in a hospital when a "code blue" message came over the public address system? Everyone who needs to know knows where to go and what to do. Everyone else goes on about their regular business less disturbed, if not undisturbed, by the announcement. This emergency plan strategy for a hospital helps them to do their job more efficiently, effectively, and smoothly. It is no different for schools.

One could envision still other situations where assistance might be needed in the classroom to handle an overly rebellious student or to take an urgent phone call down in the office. Once again, in an emergency, time is of the essence. A quickly and clearly executed emergency plan, WORKED OUT AHEAD OF TIME, can save the day.

E for Encourage vs. Praise

Encouragement is not the same thing as praise. The former stresses the activity itself, the latter the end product and, by association, the person who created the end product. Every child can be encouraged—should be encouraged—must be encouraged. A need to complete an end product, often placed in competition with other end products, severely limits the chance that every child can be the recipient of legitimate praise.

Regular encouragement is so important because of the damage that its opposite—discouragement—causes. Dinkmeyer and Dreikurs (1963, p. 42) report:

> It is incontestable that discouragement is a basic factor in all deviations, deficiencies, and failure with the exception of brain damage and mental deficiency. No one fails, with all the consequent suffering and deprivation, unless he has first lost confidence in his ability to succeed with socially accepted means. Wrongdoing takes so much persistence, endurance, and self-sacrifice, that no one would choose it unless he felt he had no alternative.

To the point of this book, discouraged children are more likely to engage in wrongdoing—misbehavior. Children who are encouraged are less likely to misbehave. So, let's offer encouragement.

Too often students evaluate themselves in terms of their achievement. They identify who they are (or are not) mainly by what they produce (Balson 1982, p. 106). Not to produce is to lack worth. To try something but not produce a valued end is to lack worth. With this in mind, students soon learn to try only those things that have a high likelihood of producing a praiseworthy result. Teachers who use praise, rather than encouragement, perpetuate the link between self-worth and achievement.

In a paper entitled, "Some Words of Encouragement," Clint Reimer (Soltz 1967, pp. 71–73) offers teachers some language for encouragement. Examples include:

1. "You do a good job of . . . ."
   This stresses the activity itself, not its finished product. Even a comment about something small and insignificant to us may have a great impact on a child.
2. "You have improved in . . . ."
   Growth and improvement are the nuts and the bolts that build student self-worth and confidence. Students may not be where we would like them to be, but if they are making progress, note that progress. It does wonders.
3. "You can help me (us, the school, and so on) by . . . ."
   To feel useful and helpful is important to everyone—including children; we have only to give them the chance.
4. "You are really working at . . . ."
   Recognition of one's diligence and persistence from teachers helps sustain learners on their way to turning an activity attempted into an activity completed. Further, these two work habits, themselves, will transfer to other endeavors.

Educators who rely upon praise soon realize that, in spite of good intentions, not everyone can be praiseworthy. In point of fact, praise loses its associated honor if too many people receive it. The Super Bowl, with all its fanfare, is designed to honor the best football team—not the one that tried the hardest, practiced the longest, was the most dedicated. There will be one and only one winner—one team worth acclaim, one team glorified. Although this may be acceptable in the world of professional sports, I question its applicability to education.

What really does praise mean in the world of education? Some student papers may be judged more praiseworthy than others, but does that mean that these same students worked harder or thought longer than others? Some students do better on exams than others, but does that mean these same students studied harder, studied longer, or appreciated more what was learned? Some student artwork may be selected for display and some not. Does that mean the students producing the selected artwork tried harder or pondered more about the project? Well, if praise carries any real meaning at all, you have to answer, "Yes." Yet, we know that in many cases the answer is "No."

Could just as much *or more* have been gained if, instead of offering praise to these students for their papers, their exams, and their artwork, we offered encouragement? I think the answer is a resounding "Yes."

Balson (1982, p. 112) summarizes his views on encouragement by noting that it "recognizes effort and improvement, shows appreciation for contribution, accepts students as they are now . . . focuses on assets and strengths, and separates the deed from the doer." Little of this can be said for offering praise.

E for Enforce, Don't Negotiate

I really never have been certain whether stores displaying the sign "You break it, you bought it!" would, or could, enforce what the sign says. The fact is, I never want to put myself in a position to find out.

Just imagine how ineffective such a statement would be if, when something was broken by a careless customer, no action was taken by the store manager. The threat or, more accurately, the logical consequence of having to pay for something that you have broken would be a hollow warning at best. Once the word got around, future customers would feel less inclined to heed the sign's warning, since the manager did not enforce store policy.

Anyone and everyone who writes on classroom management will tell you that teachers must enforce their discipline policy and must do so consistently. The more consistent the enforcement, the more the students will realize that it is the policy that triggers a teacher's disciplinary response, not the teacher himself. Discipline is seen as less personal, less up to the whim of a teacher. Students learn that it is useless to argue, useless to try to negotiate a reduced "sentence." Arguing and negotiating only have a chance of working on people, not on a discipline policy. And it is policy, assuming it is a fair policy, that is at stake here.

Don't "give in" to students who try to argue or negotiate a reduction in their punishment. Don't give in even one time. A basic understanding of operant conditioning principles, variable schedules of reinforcement in particular, tells us that even an occasional giving-in strongly encourages students' future attempts to argue or negotiate themselves out of receiving their punishment. Las Vegas casinos help create compulsive gamblers by "giving in" every once in a while and letting the customer win.

Do not listen to students' arguments and negotiating attempts. To listen is to give some possible hope. Why lead students on with false hope. Further, don't let a student's "good" behavior influence your responsibility for disciplining "bad" behavior. Some teachers let students off the hook for misbehavior that occurred during the morning *because* the students behaved themselves all afternoon. All this does is encourage children to misbehave in the earlier hours of the day.

Stand by your discipline policy. Burns (1985, p. 3) recommends that teachers make sure students "know there is a certainty that violations will be caught and dealt with." When students misbehave, they must "pay the piper." Get rid of your sense of fair play that makes you want to warn a student orally several times before you enforce the discipline policy (Morgan 1984). Once the punishment is administered, the slate, of course, is clean. If you have a discipline policy, enforce it. If you don't have a discipline policy, get one. Then enforce it!

E for Modify Environment

The best classroom management techniques are those that prevent problems from occurring in the first place. Modifying your classroom environment can provide this "ounce (or more) of prevention."

In both his *Parent Effectiveness Training* and *Teacher Effectiveness Training*, Thomas Gordon identifies and explains six different environmental modification techniques. These include Enriching and/or Impoverishing, Enlarging and/or Restricting, and Rearranging and/or Simplifying. As I briefly present Gordon's explanations of these environmental modification techniques, you might say, "I have done most of these." You are probably right—most effective teachers have made one or more of these environmental changes.

The value of repeating Gordon's definitions for these strategies is not to remember when we DID them, but to prompt our thinking about how we could consciously DO them in the future to improve classroom discipline.

Try Enriching the environment. Uninteresting environments are dull and uninspiring. They are boring. They contribute to mental idleness—the basis of the so-called "devil's workshop." Enriching consists not only of sprucing-up the physical environment (bulletin board, walls, colors), but also what is happening in the environment (speakers, varied teaching techniques).

Other times you may want to head off discipline problems by Impoverishing the environment—making it less stimulating, less interesting, less prone to attention and investigation. Checkout counters at local discount stores (for example, K-Mart) are lined with temptation. Kids pester parents, parents get mad or give in, and so the story goes—all because too much was out and readily available. "Out of sight, out of mind," works as well in a classroom environment as it does in the world of love. Try creating study carrels, quiet areas, soft music (white noise) areas. Avoid scheduling classes in areas where distractions will likely occur. Sometimes, less is really more—more learning can often take place in the midst of less stimulation.

We all know the value of Enlarging the environment. A poster on the bulletin board outside of my office reads, "The real world is outside!" suggesting that there is more to learning than just what exists within the four walls of a classroom. One of my favorite scenes in *To Sir with Love*, starring Sydney Poitier, is when he took his East End London secondary students on a field trip to a nearby museum. He enlarged their environment. Look at learning within the *confines* of a classroom as sometimes just that—confining. What experiences in your area could you make available to your students, whether you go there OR they come to you, to enlarge their environment.

There are also times when Restricting the environment can contribute to better classroom discipline. Out-of-bounds areas, prescribed areas, noise levels of students' conversations, designated painting areas, access to expensive computers, and so on, all qualify. When Restricting the environment, it would be a good idea to explain just why everyone's quality of school life will be enhanced by such moves. Don't simply dictate these limits.

Try Rearranging the environment. Not only is it sometimes more interesting than before, a plus in and of itself, it can head off trouble. Physical education classes (along with last minute showers) scheduled at one end of the building will most assuredly make it difficult for students to make it to their next class if it is scheduled on the other side of the building—hence tardiness; hence confrontations; hence trouble. Sharpening pencils *after* an exam has started will probably lead to problems also.

Where possible, Simplify the environment. One needs only to observe Montessori children in their "Casa dei Bambini," or children's house, in order to understand how many problems can be eliminated by simplifying the environment. Child-sized chairs and tables, materials placed at children's height, and carpet squares to designate private work space all simplify the environment. Look at the students' world from their eyes. What could you do (unlike the government's effort to redesign the income tax forms) to make things more simple for you and for the students?

McDaniel (1986), in a recent *Phi Delta Kappan* article, does a good job of highlighting many of these same possible environmental controls.

E for Extinguish Unwanted Behaviors

"If Sam or Mary would just stop doing such and such, my life as a teacher would be so much more pleasant." There is no doubt that if students would only stop doing some of the things they do, there would be fewer discipline problems, and thus a teacher's life would be more pleasant. What teachers would like to do is to extinguish certain student behaviors. But how?

If there is anything about operant conditioning principles that you can believe in, it is that the only way you can truly extinguish behavior is to make sure that it is no longer reinforced! Students, like the rest of us, act in a rational manner most of the time. We are purposeful in our behavior. We do things for a reason. If a student's misbehavior actually reaps him a reward, then that misbehavior is reinforced—it is more likely to occur in the future.

A student who acts up in class and, as a result, receives the attention of his peers, is rewarded for his actions. The same student who is successful in "keeping the teacher busy with him" may be similarly rewarded. The student who is able to "take" your best swats of the paddle may receive a reward from his classmates—their admiration and awe. The child who can't seem to do the assignment on his own, may be rewarded with being specially tutored by a teacher's aide. The student who seems ill prepared when answering, may be rewarded by not being so frequently called upon in the future. The examples go on and on.

It is so, so easy to "accidentally" or "unconsciously" reinforce the very student behavior you would like to extinguish. Teachers must look carefully at what precedes, what surrounds, *and* what follows a student's misbehavior for any signs that that unwanted behavior is being rewarded. To the extent possible, contributing antecedents, environmental conditions, and/or consequences must be changed.

Gnagey (1975, p. 20) argues that the teacher statement, "Don't pay any attention to him, he's just showing off," illustrates that ignoring misbehavior that is not dangerous to a student or to his classmates is likely to result in its extinction. The ignored behavior results in no student payoff.

Some teachers try to extinguish unwanted behavior by using punishment—equivalent to using a water-type fire extinguisher on an electrical fire. At first it seems to work—the flames diminish. Unfortunately, the minute you turn your head, the fire starts right up again. Get to the source of the fire—the source of the unwanted behavior. Use the correct "fire extinguisher." Determine what is reinforcing the student's undesirable behavior. Remove that reinforcement. This, and only this, will result in extinction!

E for Eye Messages

This suggestion deals with teachers using nonverbal, in most cases less disrupting, methods of classroom management. A person's eyes, in particular, can be very communicative. A glance across the classroom at a misbehaving child, followed by momentary eye contact, can stop the misbehavior in its tracks—all without any disturbance to the rest of the class. Eye Messages are equally capable of "sending" messages of approval, acceptance, and empathy.

Wolfgang and Glickman (1980, p. 21) offer "silently looking on" as one of seven typical techniques teachers use in dealing with misbehavior. Silently looking on is their equivalent to sending Eye Messages. In practice, teachers might: (1) simply look over at the offender, as if to say, "I see what you're doing but I know that you can take care of yourself," (2) observe the behavior and collect information on the entire situation before acting, or (3) gaze directly at the student with a penetrating frown.

Silently looking on is just as appropriate a tool for teachers who

believe in intervention as it is for teachers who practice nonintervention. It all depends upon how one goes about sending Eye Messages.

Although some teachers send Eye Messages better than others do, it is a skill that can be practiced and perfected. You might invite a fellow teacher to observe your class and report upon how effectively you use Eye

Messages. Do you "favor" one side of the room or direct your attention to just the front or back of the room with your Eye Messages (eye contact)? Do you stare more or less directly ahead, perhaps over the heads of your students? Although this may be a successful, anxiety-reducing suggestion offered in the past by speech teachers, it is not a successful technique for showing who is in charge.

When Eye Messages are combined with other nonverbal gestures such as an index finger raised to the lips signaling "quiet," an open hand moving up and down signaling "settle down," or a raised eyebrow signaling "disapproval," they can be very effective in maintaining classroom discipline.

The use of Eye Messages (eye contact) also has a lot to do with increasing the effectiveness of delivered consequences. Mendler and Curwin (1983, p. 143) suggest that when you repeat a rule or deliver a consequence to a student, "look directly into the eyes of the student and capture his eyes with yours. After you have finished delivering your message, maintain eye contact for a second or two and continue to maintain it as you slowly move away."

Eye Messages, with or without words, can be very, very powerful. Practice sending them. Get good at it! Having said this, one must also be conscious of the cultural diversity that exists in many of today's classrooms. Certain Eastern cultures such as Lao, Korean, and Chinese, may view direct eye contact as an expression of disrespect to adults. Be sensitive to such cultural diversity.

F for Friendly vs. Friends

There is a difference between being friendly and being friends. I recommend that you be friendly with your students but not be friends with them. Keep a "professional distance" between YOU (the teacher) and THEM (the students). This is especially important for new teachers—those without a reputation already established. Students do not have a crystal ball; they have only your behaviors from which to infer your motives. Don't provide them with behaviors from which they might infer the wrong motives.

Students already have friends. In most cases they do not need you as still one more friend—at least in the same sense that they view their other friends. Their friends, usually their peers, are very special to them and serve a unique support function in their lives now and in the future. Parents (guardians), too, are unique and serve a special support role. Teachers have a role to play in a student's life, and it is one that is different from that of the student's peers or parents. Blurring this distinction can cause problems for teachers when they are called upon to establish and maintain classroom discipline.

Teachers must keep in mind the primary reason for which they have been hired—to "keep the learning act afloat." This is what teachers, as professionals, should do best. Otherwise, why hire them? Part of the job of teaching is establishing and maintaining classroom management. This can be made more difficult if students perceive you as their friend, for, in most instances, friends do not have to manage others. Friends do not have to tell other friends to "sit down and get to work." Friends do not normally assign other friends homework. Friends normally do not formally evaluate other friends' work. The examples are endless.

Student teachers, and sometimes even new teachers, are tempted to be the students' "friend." The student teacher might see the students as a welcome refuge in a world dominated by university supervisors and cooperating teachers who, in the end, must submit a letter grade evaluating his or her performance. Avoid the temptation to become the students' friend.

Dress professionally. Act professionally. Have in mind your objectives for the day and how you plan to accomplish them. Do not permit students to call you by your first name. You may wish to return the courtesy by calling them "Mr." or "Miss." Do not go to student parties. Do not drive students to or from school. Be mindful of telling or listening to student jokes—especially if they are off-color or of an ethnic or racial nature. Too often, jokes stress little else. Do not continue to engage in conversations that appear to treat you as "one of them" and teachers as "one of some other group." That is not how it is. Don't mislead students into thinking otherwise.

Students should be mindful that things they tell their friends might stop right there; things they tell you may, in fact, be passed along. Teachers, unlike friends, often have a responsibility under the law to forward certain kinds of information (for example, child abuse, drugs, and so on) to the proper authorities. The problem here is that if students think of you as their friend and they tell you things they think will be held in confidence, your "betrayal" (in their minds) will seriously undermine the teacher/student relationship necessary for effective learning to occur.

When given an assignment to scan the suggestions in Chapter II of this book and to identify two that they would like to work on first, my sophomore-level students who are just about to start their semester-long field experience in a local school, repeatedly single out this suggestion. Many students recall how previous teaching/counseling experiences, at church or at camp, have led to disaster when they became so much a friend that their ability to lead was compromised.

Be friendly! But, do not try to be a student's friend.

G for Don't Hold a **G**rudge

Related to "Don't Take It *Personally*," a suggestion presented later, is "Don't Hold a Grudge." If a student misbehaves, deal with that misbehavior in a calm, confident, and fair manner. Discipline the child according to the offense committed. Supply your logical consequences. That should be — that *must* be — the end of it, though. The slate should be wiped clean. "The more your past mistakes are held against you, the harder it is to summon up the energy to do well now" (Glasser 1986, pp. 35 – 36). Whether referring to one's previous academic failures or to one's previous behavior patterns, the past is the past — now is now.

We all hear of the trouble people experience when they have served a jail sentence and paid their debt to society. No one ever lets them forget the fact that they have "misbehaved." Unlike exprisoners, students can't so readily move to a different city or state, change their name, and start again. You can't do a whole lot about society's reactions to exprisoners, but you can do one heck of a lot about how you treat a student offender once he has paid his debt to society.

Bartosh and Barilla (1985) make the same point but use slightly different language. They tell educators to avoid the once-a-thief-always-a-thief syndrome.

Avoid holding a grudge!

H for Seal It with a Handshake

Although this suggestion is presented in the Chapter III article, "Glasser's Reality Therapy," the idea is so important that it also bears mentioning here. This suggestion deals with the teacher and the student's sealing a bargain, a contract, a plan to which they have agreed. The agreed-upon bargain, contract, or plan most often relates to a student's commitment to a plan for improved behavior. A handshake is the tangible symbol that both parties offer their blessing and support to this plan. A handshake identifies the point between the planning stage (now recognized as being over) *and* the carrying out stage (now recognized as ready to begin).

Although you might simply ask a student to verbalize his/her commitment, the commitment is more likely to be kept if it is acknowledged in some formal fashion. Appeal to the student's sense of honor. It is said that "a man's (or woman's) handshake once was as good as his (her) word." If there is any truth to this statement, then it may well work with students, too. A handshake could be the it-has-my-blessing statement that follows a simple written contract for improved behavior prepared and signed by both the teacher and the student.

A handshake can have other value, too, if correctly executed. It is an up-front and personal gesture that can say "Welcome," "I am glad to have you here," or "We are in this together." It can be used to strengthen verbal messages that are delivered. Telling a student that his efforts have really contributed to the successful completion of a class project *and* shaking his hand at the same time increase the effect of the teacher-delivered encouragement. If performed properly, a handshake conveys sincerity. Used car salesmen, politicians, and clergy, among others, have long known this to be true.

Finally, a warm handshake can bring two human beings closer together. In schools, for legal or other reasons, and for better or worse, touching students is almost a lost art. It is often a definite "no-no." Although I do not believe a handshake is a substitute for the warmth and caring that a properly intentioned and delivered good-old hug conveys, it may be the best we can offer in today's schools. Don't overlook the power of a handshake.

I for **I**gnore Inappropriate Behavior

All behavior, including misbehavior, has a social purpose, or so say many educators (see the Chapter III article, "Dreikurs's Goals of Misbehavior"). I agree. Often that purpose is to gain attention. Therefore, if a student's misbehavior is successful in gaining attention from his teacher (or from his peers), then one would expect that misbehavior to increase in the future. A more appropriate teacher response, where possible, would be to ignore the inappropriate behavior. The words "where possible" refer to the teacher's making a judgment that the student's misbehavior is unlikely to cause himself or those around him any immediate harm.

Let me cite an example. In the 1988 Summer Olympics in Seoul, a Korean boxer lost a controversial decision. A near riot almost transpired as the Korean boxer's cornermen stormed the ring to attack the New Zealand referee. When the ruckus had ended, the NBC camera revealed that the Korean boxer was still in the middle of Ring B—just sitting there—apparently as a protest to the decision. And there he sat as the minutes ticked by. Given that there were two rings available for use, the officials decided simply to Ignore the Misbehavior and let the Korean boxer sit there. The remaining morning matches were rescheduled to Ring A. Once these matches were complete, the lights were turned off, and all spectators went home. Sixty-seven minutes after the Korean started his protest he, too, got up and left. What was the use in sitting there, misbehaving, if no one was paying attention? This is the key element that makes Ignore the Misbehavior work—whether at the Olympics or in a classroom.

In order to successfully Ignore Misbehavior, teachers must be aware of several points. One, misbehavior is likely to increase in intensity before it decreases. The student who has a habit of hollering out answers without first being called upon, may very well increase this behavior when the teacher first begins to ignore the behavior. The child reasons, "If hollering out answers a little bit no longer gets the teacher's attention, then maybe hollering out answers a lot will." Soon, though, the student realizes that his behavior of hollering out answers will no longer gain him attention. He now reasons, "What's the use in continuing a behavior that no longer gets results." His misbehavior stops.

A second point teachers need to be aware of when Ignoring Misbehavior is to reinforce behaviors that are incompatible with the misbehavior. Ignoring a student who has a tendency to wander about the classroom works well. Ignoring is far more effective if, at the same time, the teacher praises the misbehaving student when he is engaging in behaviors incompatible with the misbehavior—for example, sitting in his seat. Given that it is impossible to be sitting in one's seat *and* up wandering about the classroom, this double-barreled approach really works wonders.

■ for Send ■-Messages, Not You-Messages

How do you respond when students are misbehaving? It is tempting either to do something to make them stop their misbehavior *or* to do nothing and simply look the other way. In the first case, the teacher "wins," and the student "loses." In the second case, the student "wins," and the teacher "loses." These two common teacher responses to student misbehavior are known, respectively, as "fighting back" and "giving in."

Are these two win/lose responses the only ways a teacher can respond to student misbehavior? I hope not, because both require that one person wins at the expense of another. "Fighting back," sometimes known as "showing him who is boss," too often teaches students an unintended lesson —it is the strong people in this world who win. It teaches, by example, that the way to win in a struggle is to do so at another's expense. One can just picture a teacher shaking his finger at a student while, in effect, saying he had better do such and such or else! "Giving in" as a teacher response is no better. It also teaches an unintended lesson—my needs (student's) are more important than the needs of others. Such lessons can cause students real problems in their future interpersonal relationships.

I-Messages are an alternative teacher response to "fighting back" or "giving in." They present a win/win situation and, as such, reduce the danger that the relationship between the teacher and the student will be damaged.

I-Messages assume that the student has no particular need to continue his/her disruptive behavior and, *if given the opportunity,* will voluntarily stop that behavior. They increase the chances that students will *willingly* alter their misbehavior. Unfortunately, too many teachers give students a reason to continue their misbehavior—they tell, more often order or demand, students to stop their behavior! This inappropriate, as well as ineffective, teacher response is called a "You-Message." You-Messages do not work.

I-Messages contain three parts: a nonblameful description of the student's behavior, the tangible effect now or in the future that the behavior is having on you, and the feeling that tangible effect is causing you. A clear description of the misbehavior is required in order to be sure that both of you are concentrating upon the same behavior. The description should be nonblameful in order to reduce the likelihood that the student will feel he is being attacked or being judged.

Identifying a tangible effect makes it apparent that the student's actions are affecting you in a concrete, recognizable way. Students, as well as others, are more likely to change their behavior voluntarily if it is clearly shown that their behavior is tangibly affecting you. Describing the feeling you are experiencing helps to reinforce the tangible effect the student's behavior is having on you. Note, the whole focus of the I-Message is on you, not on the student. As a result, there is less chance that the student will feel a need to be defensive.

Let me offer an example of a classroom situation followed by a teacher-delivered I-Message. See if you can identify the three parts of a properly stated I-Message. Try to envision what the student's response might be.

> It is almost time for the mock fire drill scheduled for 2:00 P.M. Your second-graders are required to go outside and stand in their designated spot until everyone is accounted for. Because the weather is cold and rainy, you have asked your students to put their raincoats and boots on ahead of time. It is 1:58 P.M., and David has yet to get dressed. You are ready to "wring his neck."
>
> I-Message: "David, when you do not have your raincoat and boots on and it is almost time for our scheduled fire drill (nonblameful description), we will not be able to get to our assigned spot on time (tangible effect), and I am afraid that the principal will think I am not a responsible teacher (feeling)."

Are I-Messages effective with all misbehaving students? No. But remember that our goal is to use classroom management techniques that work with most students, most of the time, in most situations. I-Messages are "more appropriate for the normally self-disciplined student who is acting on impulse, spontaneously, and thoughtlessly" (Shrigley 1985, p. 29). These messages work best when the teacher has a rapport established with a particular student—the teacher is a "significant other" in the student's life.

I-Messages do not tell the student how he should modify his behavior in order to satisfy you. Instead, I-Messages simply note the effect of his behaviors on you and how you feel as a result. The rest is up to the student. He is left to his own initiative to "put on a white hat" and become the "good guy" by voluntarily changing his behavior. How much better it is when a student responds out of respect for you, for the rapport the two of you have, than it is when a student is forced to respond out of fear of you. For those students with whom you have developed some sense of rapport, I-Messages work great.

See the Chapter III article, "Gordon's Teacher (Parent) Effectiveness Training," for more information on I-Messages.

I for Identify Specific Misbehaviors

Before any classroom management strategy can be successful in changing a student's behavior, that behavior must first be identified. This is the only way it can work. Specific behaviors must be targeted, for it

is only specific behaviors, not general characteristics, that one can hope to change.

Saying that a student is "uncooperative," "a troublemaker," "undependable," or "immature" doesn't tell you a thing! These terms mean different things to different people. A child's refusing to follow directions could be seen by one teacher as "uncooperative," and by another teacher as "independent." What matters here is not which teacher is correct but what SPECIFIC BEHAVIORS of the student led both teachers to their general conclusion. It is only these specific behaviors that may be increased, maintained at the present level, or decreased. This is really your goal. Therefore, make specific observable behaviors your focus.

If Johnny is labeled a "troublemaker" as a result of regularly striking fellow students when out on the playground for recess, then the targeted behavior in need of correction is his "striking fellow students," not the summary label of being a "troublemaker." Ask yourself, "What is the student doing that leads you (and perhaps others) to label him as a troublemaker?" In this case it is hitting other students. Once you are successful in getting him to stop striking fellow students (targeted behavior), then the label of "troublemaker" will no longer apply. No matter what classroom management techniques you decide to use, they must be directed at increasing, maintaining at the present level, or decreasing *specific behaviors.*

One other thing that happens when you label students is that the labels never seem to go away even when the behaviors that caused the labeling have ceased. Once called a "troublemaker," will Johnny forever be saddled with that label even when your classroom management strategies are successful in getting him to stop striking fellow students? Unfortunately, the answer is often "Yes." Avoid dealing in vague labels when describing misbehaving students. It does absolutely no good whatsoever! Instead, clearly identify the specific misbehavior, and then set about, using appropriate management strategies, to change that behavior. Period. Do it; it works.

J for Judge and Jury

I could have used "J" for Justice to title this suggestion. One thing students are looking for in a classroom is justice, equity, and/or fairness. When students perceive that justice does not exist, one can expect them to act — maybe even act out. They expect no less than we as citizens demand — even in a less than ideal world. In the world outside of the classroom, we have a court system complete with, among other designated personnel, a judge and a jury. Note that the judge is the judge, and the jury is the jury. Except in rare cases, they are not one and the same. Why not? Justice is thought to be better served by keeping the two roles separated.

What about the situation in a classroom? Teachers commonly find themselves in the role of both judge and jury when it comes to classroom management. In fact, teachers not only may be the judge and the jury, but often they are also the accuser. How would you feel going before a judge who is also both your accuser and your jury? If it appears to be a little bit rigged, it is. This stacking of the deck does not go unnoticed by students.

Take, for instance, the student who is accused of something by his teacher. How prepared is the teacher, now playing the role of judge, to ensure procedural fairness? Although one would expect the teacher, now playing the role of prosecuting attorney, to do so with spirit and determination, who will act as the student's defense attorney? The teacher? I hope not. The student? How does the saying go, "A person who acts as his own attorney has a fool for a client"? Finally, how able is the teacher, now asked to play the role of jury, to render a fair and impartial decision?

Although I do not expect that all classroom discipline problems are destined to turn into Perry Mason courtroom episodes, the point is that teachers are asked to assume several roles related to ensuring that justice is rendered. Further, the courts of our nation have traditionally had a hands-off attitude toward a school's disposition of the run-of-the-mill discipline problems. This means that educators have a good deal more leeway in their decision making when it comes to what to discipline and how to discipline.

I would ask teachers to be aware of this responsibility and, as with the suggestion, "Legitimate Power; Don't Abuse It," to keep the power that goes with this responsibility in check. Go ahead, be the judge, be the jury, but govern your actions by sound judgment.

K for **K**ounin's Withitness

Who doesn't want to be "With it"? What I am referring to here is not one's dress, hairstyle, having read the latest best seller, or using up-to-date slang. Kounin (1970) defines "withitness" as the teacher's demonstrating that she knows what is going on in her classroom. Nothing (at least little) seems to get by her. She seems to have "eyes in the back of her head." No one, but no one, can pull the "wool over her eyes"—don't even bother trying. The student's perception is that she will catch you, and she will deal with you!

With respect to classroom management, teachers with withitness demonstrate proper target identification and timing when supplying "desists" (procedures designed to stop behavior). Target identification refers to catching the correct culprit, disciplining the right misbehaving child. If more than one child is misbehaving or if onlookers and imitators have appeared, the withitness teacher singles out the central figure, the instigator. Identifying the wrong student and, even worse, punishing the wrong student seriously undermine one's effectiveness and credibility as a disciplinarian. Teachers who are able to clearly identify appropriate offenders, while at the same time avoiding involving innocent bystanders, are preferred by students (Lewis and Lovegrove 1984). Although when mistaken identifications are made, they may be "defended" as one of those great lessons in life (the world is not perfect), few children appreciate this message. They see the situation, and you, as unaware and unfair.

Withitness teachers also demonstrate proper timing. They execute their classroom management strategy before the deviant behavior spreads and increases in seriousness. A simple kitchen fire extinguisher can, if used early enough, stop a catastrophic fire. But, if one waits too long to intervene, that same simple fire extinguisher will be useless. It is no different in classroom management.

Although it may take a little time and energy to establish one's self as possessing "withitness," that reputation can go a long way toward discouraging discipline problems from occurring. The payoff is more time and energy left to teach and for children to learn. Be withit!

L for Legitimate Power; Don't Abuse It

As a teacher, you have at least five social bases of power available. Legitimate power, sometimes referred to as authority, is one of these five. You may think you have authority over students simply because you have been hired as their teacher. In fact, legitimate power exists only because students perceive that you have the right to dictate portions of their behavior—within defined parameters. If their perceptions change, you may no longer have that power.

You can assign homework, and, except for a few groans here and there, you can expect that most students will comply. As a teacher, you have the right to assign homework! You can, among many legitimate teacher actions, break students into groups, have them take tests, require speeches and term papers, and assign grades. All of these "rights" come with the territory.

A problem occurs when teachers exceed the boundaries of their authority and make *illegitimate* demands upon students. In such situations the bold students will let you know they believe you have exceeded your legitimate power. Cutting into the cafeteria line in front of hungry students, telling students for whom they should vote, demanding that students get their hair cut, may all bring the comment, "Just because you are the teacher, that does not give you the right to. . . ." And, you know, they are correct. You don't have the right, just because you are a teacher, to do or demand some of these things.

In the 1960s hit movie *To Sir with Love,* Sydney Poitier plays a teacher in an inner-city East London school where he is making real headway with students who have never valued education. An incident occurs in physical education in which an overweight student is ordered, despite his protests and those of his classmates, to leap over the vaulting horse. He attempts the jump but comes crashing down onto the floor, injuring himself. Later, in Poitier's class, the incident is discussed and one student says, "Just because Mr. Ames is the teacher, it doesn't give him the right to force Harold to vault the horse. Harold can't do it, he is too heavy!" This teacher, at least in the eyes of the students, exceeded his legitimate power.

The statement, "Just because you are the . . . ," shows up in many walks of life, not just education, when subordinates feel their bosses have exceeded their legitimate power. In one episode of the TV hospital series, *St. Elsewhere,* Luther, the black hospital orderly, confronted the chief surgeon by saying, "Just because you are the rich, white doctor, it doesn't give you the right to say what you just said!" Luther had had enough. The chief surgeon had overstepped his legitimate power. The chief surgeon was wrong; Luther was right.

In the two examples above, the individuals affected were forward enough to voice their complaint. Once voiced, the complaint can be handled. Just think, though, of the many students out there who "think" the same complaint about teachers but don't voice it. As teachers, must we wait until the complaint is voiced, before we take corrective action? Why not take inventory of our doings and demands? Why not, where appropriate, change what we are doing and demanding if such behaviors are really illegitimate applications of our power and authority?

Remember, our goal is to improve classroom discipline. Illegitimate use of our authority undermines that discipline. It makes us appear unfair, and even worse, perhaps unaware that we are being unfair. It too often results in teachers trying to justify their demands, once illegitimately made, when everyone knows they can't really be justified. It makes teachers appear to be hiding behind the title "Teacher," as if it were a license for any behavior on their part. No one is being fooled. Don't let this happen.

As a class exercise, I asked my students to look back on their school years and complete the statement, "Just because you are the _____, that does not give you the right to. . . ." The students were instructed to refer to an illegitimate demand (from their viewpoint) of either a parent or teacher. They had no difficulty coming up with real examples. For instance, "Just because you are my parent, that does not give you the right to tell me what I can and cannot wear. I am my own person and have a right to make this decision on my own." Or, "Just because you are my parent, that does not give you the right to tell me where and when I can or cannot spend my own money. I earned it; I should decide how to spend it."

In school one may hear, "Just because you are a teacher, that does not give you the right to badger students because they do not know the answer, to the point of making them cry." Or, "Just because you are a teacher, that does not give you the right to continuously embarrass me in front of the whole class by making rude comments about my dress and my hair."

Sometimes children are right. The power that comes with our position as a parent or teacher has limits. Be aware of those limits. Do not abuse your legitimate power!

In order to "take inventory" of whether or not you may have abused your legitimate power, why not have students complete anonymously the statement, "Just because you are the teacher, that does not give you the right to. . . ." Who knows, you may get some surprise answers. If you do this exercise early enough in the semester, you can then make appropriate changes in behavior.

See the Chapter III article, "French and Raven's Social Bases of Power" for more information on this topic.

L for Legitimization: Where to Place the Sidewalks?

As the story goes, officials of a small college were trying to decide where to locate the sidewalks of a new building complex to best respond to student preferences. Should architects be consulted? Should a college-wide committee be formed? The problem was resolved by not laying any sidewalks at all—at least not at first. Instead, the buildings were opened, and students moved about creating paths that reflected their preferences. These dirt paths were then "legitimized" by being paved in concrete. The students' natural behaviors were, in effect, legitimized.

There are numerous student behaviors that occur in schools that are judged by teachers to be inappropriate. Building and throwing paper airplanes, talking to classmates, forgetting to turn in homework papers, and being late for class are examples.

Why not consider legitimizing one or more of these or other misbehaviors? Could students earn time to be used for paper airplane construction and flying? Could students earn time to chitchat with peers? The amount of time earned could be just a minute or so, yet to students it is a really big deal. Can students earn a token that they can turn in for one forgotten homework paper or for one time being late to class? The common element here is to "earn" these rights legitimately to engage in what would otherwise be misbehavior.

Students might earn five minutes of paper airplane flying contest time each week by *not* flying paper airplanes any other time during the week. Students may earn time to chitchat with peers by *not* doing it during other times throughout the week. They could earn a forgotten-homework token by having homework in for a specific number of days in a row. The same strategy could be used for earning a late-to-class token. If you can't stop certain illegitimate behavior, then make it legal. Making it legal makes the behavior less attractive in the first place.

When I think of a typical schoolteacher's contract, I note a common inclusion of personal days—perhaps two a year. Are these not the school district's attempt to legitimize what would otherwise be teacher misbehavior—teachers not coming to school and yet not being ill?

As a final example of legitimizing behavior, I offer state lotteries. Those states having lotteries could have spent endless hours, person-power, and resources trying to stop gambling by their citizens. Instead, these states made the misbehavior legal with the end result being that the state has regained some control over the "misbehavior." These states have also made lots of money from legalizing this form of gambling—much of which goes to education and to the elderly.

Be creative. Think of how you can curtail those unwanted behaviors by legitimizing them.

L for Listen to Your Students

Everyone, at one time or another, needs someone to listen to them. Children have no less a need. Teachers are often in the best position to provide a pair of willing ears, a shoulder to cry on, an empathetic nod or grunt. It can do wonders.

Listening to students is time well spent, for it is unlikely that they will be able to attend properly to the instructional tasks at hand *until* they have talked out their problem with someone. I know, for one, I can't. If you don't take the time to listen to students, then they will seek out other listeners—a friend in the hallway, a student across the aisle. When this happens, students often can get themselves into trouble. They are penalized for being late for class, are accused of talking in class, trying to get answers from other students, disturbing fellow students, and so on. All this because they had a need to talk to someone about a problem they were experiencing.

When listening to students, the teacher's goal ought not be to solve the student's problem for him. Sometimes problems have no solution—for example, a grandmother dies, a pet runs away, parents split up. What is far more important is that the child be given the opportunity to talk out the strong, and often debilitating, feelings he has concerning the problem. As a teacher, you can provide that opportunity.

Although the problems students commonly face may not seem earth-shaking to us, they can seem that way to them. An effective listener shows respect for the problems of others—big and small. Nothing shows more respect for another person's problem than to resist the urge to add one's "two cents."

Sometimes the circumstances are positive ones—the child now has a new baby sister, the entire family went to Sea World over the weekend, the family dog just had puppies. These examples become problems for a student when they stir such emotions that he can't productively do anything else until he tells someone his news. He is simply bursting at the seams to tell someone!

Be empathetic, but do not give license for wrongdoing with that empathy. It is easy to subtly, and unintentionally, reinforce inappropriate behavior by seeming to agree with a listener (Britton and Stallings 1981, p. 63). Empathizing does not mean agreeing. Listening to a student *does not* and *should not* necessarily mean that you agree with what the student is saying. That should be made very clear.

When a student gets a gripe off his chest about the school principal or speaks in rather negative terms about the recently increased graduation requirements, it would not be proper nor helpful for a teacher to agree or disagree. Instead, noncommittal responses such as, "No kidding," "My my," "You don't say," "Hummm," "You feel pretty strongly about that," and even a nonverbal nod, all convey a message that you are listening and that you are keeping pace with what he is saying. You, in effect, are grunting or nodding at the right time and with the right intensity. The ball is left in the hands of the student to keep talking or to decide he has said enough and, at least for now, to put his problem aside and get on with his schoolwork.

Being an effective listener does not come easily to some people. This is especially true for teachers who may see their primary role as disseminating information. I read somewhere that eighty percent of the time someone is talking in the classroom, and eighty percent of that time it is the teacher doing the talking.

Specific listening skills need to be learned and then practiced. In Thomas Gordon's book, *Teacher Effectiveness Training* (1974), he describes a model that identifies twelve "roadblocks" to effective listening that are commonly used by even the best intentioned of us. Among these are giving shoulds and oughts, advising, offering solutions, giving logical arguments, agreeing, interpreting, analyzing, reassuring, sympathizing, and questioning.

Gordon goes on to identify and explain alternative listening skills including: silence, noncommittal responses, door openers, and active listening. Active listening is Gordon's down-to-earth application of Carl Rogers's reflective counseling. See the Chapter III article, "Gordon's Teacher (Parent) Effectiveness Training," for a more detailed discussion of these skills.

Taking the time *and* having the skills to listen to students who are experiencing problems pays great dividends. At a minimum, it heads off possible discipline problems. It is, like so many other effective classroom management strategies, a preventive measure.

Finally, listening to students should not be seen as a contradiction to the *"Friendly vs. Friends"* suggestion. Friendly teachers can listen.

M for **M**r. or **M**iss

Do children act any differently when they are dressed in their Sunday-go-to-meeting clothes than when they are in their dungarees? Often, the answer is yes. Wearing good clothes signals a special event that warrants special behavior. An expectation is established that is, more often than not, lived up to.

Addressing students by "Mr." or "Miss" can form similar expectations that can also be lived up to by one's behaviors. When students are addressed as Mr. or Miss, a feeling of being more grown up is generated. What child does not want to be perceived as grown-up? But, being treated as a grown-up doesn't come free. Students can understand that. It carries with it responsibilities that did not need to be shouldered when one was addressed simply as "Johnny," "Wendy," or "Bobby." The title Mr. or Miss conveys a trust on the part of a teacher that one is deserving of that salutation. Once again, more often than not, students will make an attempt to live up to that trust. They will act more grown-up—they will misbehave less often.

Chances are, other teachers have not addressed students as Mr. or Miss. You, then, are doing something different, something special. This action will not go unnoticed by the children. Students like to "get even," "set the scorecard straight," "put things back in balance." How can they do this? Most likely, they will reciprocate the respect you have shown them.

There is one caution to keep in mind when using this suggestion. Be careful of the tone of your voice. In the past, some teachers have reserved calling students "Mr." or "Miss" for when they wanted to use the title as a put-down. For example, "Well, MISS BUTLER, let's hear what you might have to say on the subject!" If you call students by "Mr." or "Miss," only do so out of respect. After all, that is how you would prefer they use your title.

N for Learn Their Names

Learn the students' names as quickly as possible. This is a must. Many classroom management techniques, as well as teaching techniques, are enhanced by knowing a student's name. It allows you to direct your comments to specific students regardless of whether you have eye contact with them or not. We all know the ease with which a misbehaving student (possibly sitting in the back of the room, whispering to a neighbor) can be brought back into the mainstream of a class discussion simply by directing a question in his direction. Since he is apparently paying no attention to the class discussion, you will obviously need to address him by name.

Do not take more than two days to learn students' names. You simply cannot afford to have many incidents occur in which you have to say, "Hey you, quiet down," or "Hey, what's-your-name, what do you think the author meant by. . . ?" The kind of "testing" answer you may very well receive, and one you don't want, is one such as, "Who, me?" or "Are you talking to me?" This challenging situation is easily avoided by calling a student by name. Then there is no question who your comment was directed toward. How you handle yourself in the first few days, and how much or how little students find they can get away with, are crucial to establishing discipline for the rest of the year.

Consider having 4″ by 6″ name card "tents" that students place on their desks. Consider having students complete some sort of background information form or nongraded pretest that keeps them occupied while you move up and down the rows learning their names. Little is more impressive to students than when, at the end of a period, you ask them to

look up at you while you identify each of them by name. Seating charts
can be a big help. Practice associating students' features with their names.
Who has a Scottish name and has red hair? Does Linda over there look a
lot like someone you know named Linda? I don't care how you learn their
names, just do it. Do it as soon as possible. The students will be in awe.
They will wonder if you know this much about them already, what else do
you know about them. It keeps them guessing.

There once was the story of the college student taking a final exam in
a room with 300 other students. The professor saw the student cheating.
When the student went to turn in his exam, the professor said, "I can't
accept that exam, you cheated." The student looked at the pile of over 200
exams that had already been submitted, and asked the professor, "Do you
know my name?" The professor said "No," and the student quickly slid
his exam into the pile of already submitted tests and quickly exited stage
left. What could the professor do? Nothing.

N for Personal Needs: Yours and Theirs

When you prepare for that Saturday garage sale by pricing all of those
"treasures," it is important to consider what's the least money you will
accept—your bottom line. One can really be taken advantage of and,
more importantly, FEEL taken advantage of, if you don't think about the
"least you will be satisfied with" until it is too late. It is no different in
education.

Teachers should decide ahead of time what are their *minimum*
needs—those student behaviors that must be met before they can get on
with effective teaching. These needs should be kept to a minimum, should
be clearly communicated to students, should be defended as with a "cause
and effect" argument, and should be consistently enforced. Canter and
Canter (1976) suggest that it is the assertive teacher who gets his needs
met first and then goes on to act in the best interest of his students.
Whether you consider yourself to be assertive or not, it is important to
identify your minimum prerequisite needs.

Do you have a need for students to arrive at class on time, to have
pencils ready and books open when the bell rings, to complete assigned
homework, to raise their hands before speaking, to keep books properly
covered, to. . . ? What student behaviors are really, really important to
you? Think about the answer to this question now.

Don't assume students know what is important to you, what "bugs"
you. Your minimum prerequisite needs may be similar or different from
those of other teachers. It makes no difference. Determine, convey,
defend, and enforce your minimum needs.

Listen to your kids. Listen to them as they express their needs. When
possible, respond. Children, just like you, CANNOT meet their own
deficiency needs—safety, love and belonging, and esteem. They need
help—often your help. By the way, you can't meet your own deficiency
needs either. You, too, need help. Often, given the nature of your job, that

help can come from students. It looks as if students and teachers are in a position to help each other meet their respective needs!

O for Organized and Overlapping

As cited in the literature, one of the most common characteristics of a successful teacher is that of being organized. Teachers must organize people, materials, time, activities, and lessons. Organizing any one of these things could be a full-time job. Trying to organize all of them at once, especially when there is an interaction among them, takes superhuman effort. Yet, most successful teachers make it look easy.

Feedback from over 500 of my sophomore Educational Psychology students who took part in a semester-long field experience in local schools offers firsthand acknowledgement of the necessity for requisite organizational skills. These preservice teachers never ceased to be amazed at how things went like clockwork in their cooperating teachers' classrooms. Students were where they were supposed to be, and they were there on time; materials were available and distributed with little or no fuss; time was allocated effectively; activities were precisely coordinated; and lessons for individuals, as well as groups, were designed and delivered. Added to this were all the unexpected events that had to be handled without disturbing the established organization.

One key element in being organized is the ability to handle overlapping situations (Kounin 1970). It simply is not possible for a teacher to address just one thing at a time, dispense with it, AND THEN move onto something else. I once worked part-time in a small college town restaurant. On weekends the owner, whom I'll call Mrs. Jones, did the cooking. She would cook one order at a time—period. Even when I submitted four or five orders, each for two fried eggs, toast, and bacon, she still cooked one order at a time. It took forever. Customers got mad. Customers got unruly; they caused the restaurant the equivalent of "discipline problems." All of this difficulty could have been avoided had Mrs. Jones been able to take care of more than one thing at a time—handle overlapping events.

I was in a classroom recently where the children were "celebrating" a Scandinavian holiday. Tradition has it that the oldest daughter (oldest female in class) and the youngest son (youngest male in class) serve the food and drink to the family (classmates). Drink had to be poured and passed out. Food had to be placed on trays and distributed. Two cups of drink spilled and had to be wiped up. Three girls working on a computer in the back of the room asked for assistance. The principal made an announcement over the public address system. And finally, I was there for a short visit with the teacher. The teacher needed overlapping skills!

Overlapping is like trying to keep several balls in the air at the same time. If too much attention is paid to one ball, the rest fall to the ground. Balls in the air, or events happening in a classroom, simply cannot be attended to one at a time.

The more organization a teacher has, and the more that she can handle overlapping events, the fewer discipline problems she will have. Even if you are not an organized person by nature, work at giving every outward appearance that you are organized. Take the time to PLAN what is going to happen in your classroom with people, material, time, activities, and lessons. Play a "what if" game with yourself. Ask yourself, "What if I have this group doing such and such, what is likely to happen with the rest of the children?" "What if we are only able to get the Thanksgiving turkeys partially cut out and glued before we run out of time?" "What if I prepared individual student folders to make it easier for students to locate their work?" Appear organized. Be organized. Plan, plan, plan. Accept the reality of overlapping events; they will not go away.

O for Over-prepare

When do students misbehave? Often, says Tenoschok (1985, p. 30), "it is when students are bored or do not have a specific task to perform." You can make sure students have something *constructive* to do by over-preparing for your lessons. As a rule, it is far better to have more planned to do than you are able to do, rather than to be caught with five or ten minutes of the period left with nothing to do. This would be just asking for problems to occur.

Beginning teachers are often asked to over-prepare their teaching assignments, at least until they have taught a lesson several times so that they can better predict just how much *can* and *should* be taught in a given period of time. Even now, after twenty years of teaching experience, I occasionally get "caught" at the end of a period.

Over-preparing not only applies to the quantity of material you plan to deliver, but also to the minimum and maximum limits of what you can effectively do with the material. Say that you glance at the clock and see that there are ten minutes left in the class period. You now have several decisions. Can the discussion of the present material last for ten minutes? Should you ask one or two more open-ended questions to extend the discussion? Can you wrap up the present material in a minute or so and effectively use the remaining eight minutes to get started on new material? Should you plan to complete the present discussion a minute or two before the end of the period and then provide two minutes of low volume talk time as a reward for their eager participation?

I don't know which of these paths you should follow. By over-preparing and thinking of alternative ways that you can use to present, shorten, or extend presentations, you will more effectively use instructional time. You will keep students on task. Fewer discipline problems are likely to occur.

There is a positive correlation between over-preparing and presenter confidence—and it shows. Teachers who know what they want to get done and who have designed relevant and interesting instructional strategies step into the classroom ready to move forward with recognizable goals in mind. They exude confidence. Confident teachers have fewer discipline problems.

By the way, over-preparing does not equate to knowing all there is to know about any given subject. No one can be that prepared. It is okay not to have all the answers. Finally, over-preparing does not mean that teachers have a right to regularly keep students beyond their allotted class time, perhaps into their lunch period, just so they can deliver all the information they over-prepared!

Over-prepare! It pays.

P for Don't Take It Personally

As hard as it might sound, don't take student misbehaviors personally. Except for the most extreme set of circumstances, one can't possibly believe that students plot for a day or so on just how to make your life more miserable. Therefore, deal with the specific misbehavior, the specific rule that has been broken, the specific discipline problem. Deal with it impartially.

It is alright for a teacher to behave in a manner showing concern, caring, and respect. It IS NOT alright, nor is it helpful in establishing and maintaining classroom discipline, to act in a disrespectful or vengeful manner.

Students who are discouraged, who feel they don't belong, who have their own personal, peer, and/or family problems may very well engage in behaviors that are deemed unacceptable. In plain terms, they may misbehave. (See the Chapter III article, "Dreikurs's Goals of Misbehavior.") Certainly do not overlook the misbehavior. It must be dealt with. At the same time, though, don't take it personally.

P for Premack Principle or Grandma's Rule

"Hey, Dad, just let me watch this television program, and then I will do my homework." "Right after I go play some tennis, I will complete that report." "Sure, I'll get the garage cleaned up, right after I get back from an afternoon at the beach." Promises, promises, promises—often unkept!

What do these at-home examples have to do with being a teacher? Well, they are presented as a frame of reference. If you can identify with these examples *and* realize how often we end up *not* doing the homework, completing the report, or cleaning the garage, then you can begin to understand why such statements lead to problems. Doing what you want to do first *and* promising to do what you would rather not do after doesn't often work. Any grandma knows this when she states the proposition, "First eat all of your dinner, and then you may have ice cream." No amount of grandchild urging will persuade her otherwise.

The Premack Principle says that one should use high frequency behaviors as a reward for low frequency behaviors. High frequency behaviors are those things the person really wants to do—watch television, play tennis, go to the beach. Low frequency behaviors are those things the person really does not want to do—do homework, complete reports, clean the garage.

No matter how good children's intentions are to live up to their word, allowing people (even yourself) to engage in the more desired high frequency behaviors first, with the promise that they will then engage in less desired low frequency behaviors, works well very rarely. As the teacher or parent, you end up having to remind, nag, and generally pester the child into living up to his end of the bargain. This strains the relationship.

Make access to the more desired high frequency behaviors CONTINGENT UPON the completion of the less desired low frequency behaviors. This way works. Tell students who would rather chat with their neighbor, "If you correctly complete the ten assigned math problems, then you will be able to chat with your neighbor for five minutes." Tell students who would rather just sit and draw pictures, "If you correctly complete the remaining three pages of your skill pack, you may have five uninterrupted minutes to draw your pictures." Tell students who just love to daydream, "If you correctly identify ninety percent of the capital cities in your map exercise, you may have ten minutes to just sit there and daydream."

Connecting the low frequency behaviors to the high frequency behaviors increases the odds that students will do the math, do their skill pack, and do their map. Try rewording the statements by allowing the high frequency behaviors first. The odds that students would complete the low frequency behaviors would be significantly reduced!

Note that in each of the three correctly worded statements I specifically defined what was expected of them when engaging in the low frequency behaviors. In each case, the low frequency behaviors must be done correctly—no rushing through in a slipshod manner. Further, exactly how much of each low frequency behavior has been defined— ten math problems, three pages of skill pack, ninety percent identification of capital cities. This is crucial. Do not simply say, "If you work on your mathematics problems FOR A WHILE, then you may talk with your neighbor."

How long is "FOR A WHILE,"—ten problems, one week, a full semester? Who knows? How long will I be able to talk with my neighbor? Fifteen seconds, one class period? Put yourself in the place of a child who is asked to do a chore. The parent says, "Work on these leaves for a while, and I'll let you play on the computer." You would like a more specific definition of what "work on" and "for a while" means. You would also want to know how much time you will get to play on the computer. Real discipline problems can occur if the two of you have different definitions for these words. Don't let this happen.

How do you know what are high frequency behaviors for each of your students? You could simply ask them ahead of time to identify their *expressed* interests. Another way to identify these behaviors is to schedule some "free time" in the students' day, sit back, and observe their *manifested* interests — what they decide to do during this free time. Record your observations for future use in forming Premack Principle contingency statements.

The Premack Principle works. It works best when the low frequency behaviors *and* the high frequency behaviors are clearly specified.

P for Punctuality

"Neither rain nor snow nor last minute copier needs nor unfinished cups of coffee shall keep me from my appointed duties." This slightly altered letter carrier oath applies just as well to teachers. You expect your students to be dependable, to be accountable, to be where they are supposed to be when they are supposed to be there. Can you expect anything less of yourself? RHIP (Rank Has Its Privileges) as a reason (excuse) for not being on time ought to be used sparingly. Just think how much one may appear to be a hypocrite if one demands behaviors of others that one is unwilling to model oneself. It is a poor leader who does not hold himself up to the same standards as those he leads.

Enough of the preaching. The fact is, when students are left unsupervised, you are just asking for trouble. It is during this time that they are more prone to act out, to act up, to act differently than when they are at task under the supervision of an appropriate adult. For every discipline problem that does not occur because you are where you are supposed to be, when you are supposed to be, that is one less time you will have to use classroom management strategies.

Is this to say that students are incapable of self-supervision? Of course not. In fact, more and more self-supervision (self-discipline) is just what we would hope would emerge over a student's years in school. The difference, though, is that self-supervision is something that should be planned. For instance, students could be told ahead of time that you will be late for a class and asked to get on with their assigned tasks. Here it may be fair to hold them accountable.

This is very different from simply not showing up on time and expecting students to go on as if you were there. The popular television public service spot that says, "It's ten P.M. Do you know where your children are?" speaks for teachers as well. It is the start of second period, do you know where your students are, *and* what they are doing? You should. If you are where you are supposed to be—on time—you can answer, "Yes!"

This reminds me of a story. A new teacher showed up late to her third-floor classroom only to see a student sitting on the window ledge with his legs dangling outside! The teacher screamed at him to "get back in here immediately!" She followed with a discourse on how he could have been killed had he fallen to the cement pavement below. Later, in the teachers' room she confessed to a fellow teacher that what had really worried her was how she would have explained to the principal and the child's parents just how the student had had the time and opportunity to be out on the ledge in the first place. What possible excuse could she have had, had the accident happened, for not being at her assigned post? None!

Be where you are supposed to be, and be there on time. Don't be caught in the position of having to defend the undefendable. Besides, the more you are where you are supposed to be, the more constructive learning should take place. That's the bottom line.

P for **P**unishment; In Practice, Who Really Supports It?

Of the four consequences available to teachers in operant conditioning (positive reinforcement, negative reinforcement, punishment, and time-out), none has been written about more than has punishment. For example, a review of articles indexed in *Psychological Abstracts* from 1980 to 1985 revealed over 350 citations with punishment in the title (Tauber 1988). This was twice the number of citations as for positive reinforcement, its nearest competitor. In a DIALOG search of Educational Resources Information Center (ERIC) from 1966 to 1987, 275 titles with punishment in the title were cited, five times the number cited which had positive reinforcement in the title (Tauber 1988).

With all of this information on punishment available, educators should be in a position to take an unwavering stand on whether or not punishment has a place in a school. Unfortunately, such is not the case.

As a regular classroom (as well as in-service workshop) exercise on the topic of punishment, the author asks his audience, "In *general,* how many of you see a place for punishment's being supplied in the schools?" Without exception, at least eighty percent of the hands are raised in agreement. At this point, *specific* examples of punishment are identified.

The specific examples of punishment used are those identified by Mager (1968, pp. 49–60) in his chapter on aversive consequences. He lists frustration, humiliation and embarrassment, fear and anxiety, boredom, physical discomfort, and pain as all-encompassing categories of punishment. One cannot simply supply punishment; one must supply one or more specific examples of punishment.

In the order listed above, the author goes on to ask how many in the audience would "purposefully" use each of these forms of punishment. The term *purposefully* is stressed with the assumption that teachers act in a purposeful manner no matter what they do. To do otherwise would be very, very scary—to students and parents alike.

When the author asks the first question, "How many of you would purposefully plan to frustrate your students?" Few people raise their hands. Some wonder out loud how I could possibly think a teacher would purposefully do such a thing. Yet, frustrating students is a form of punishment. Presenting information at a faster pace than students can handle, teaching one set of skills and testing for another, or using materials with too high a reading level are all examples.

When the audience is asked, "How many of you would purposefully plan to humiliate and embarrass your students?" only a few people respond by raising their hands. Even these people say that they would reserve such punishment for unique situations.

How does the audience respond when asked, "How many of you would purposefully plan to instill fear and anxiety in your students?" Once again, only a few hands signal, "Yes," and these go up ever so slowly. Instilling fear and anxiety seems to be less than acceptable teacher behavior.

When I ask, "How many of you would purposefully plan to come in and bore your students?" the audience breaks out in nervous laughter. Yet, no one can argue that there are few things more punishing than having to listen to someone who is boring. It hurts; it hurts a lot. The audience seems ready and willing to dismiss this category of punishment.

When I ask the audience's willingness to punish students by supplying physical discomfort, most think this means hitting or paddling the child. Of the categories of punishment asked about thus far, this one is the winner. A whopping ten percent of the hands might be raised. But once I point out that supplying physical discomfort means such things as making the room too hot or cold, having students sit in seats that are too hard, too small, too large, and so on, most of the raised hands are lowered.

Finally, I ask, "How many of you see a place for purposefully instilling pain in children?" Perhaps it's the fear of being sued, perhaps the research on corporal punishment has been read, or perhaps the teachers can picture a 185-pound man striking a little fourth-grader, and it makes them feel guilty, but for whatever the reason, no more than ten percent of the audience agrees with this form of punishment.

At this point we have a real quandary. Eighty percent or more responded in the beginning by indicating that they saw a place for punishment in the schools. Yet, when they are asked to show their support for specific categories of punishment, few raise their hands. Could it be that teachers do not really support punishment as much as they might at first have believed? After all, one cannot be for punishment *in general,* and against all *specific* examples of it.

It is my observation that, when it comes to "put up or shut up," most educators do not support specific examples of punishment. Let's not fool ourselves otherwise.

Q for Qualifier for Punishment

The best advice I could offer would be to avoid punishment in the first place. Punishment is nothing more than a contrived consequence and is really not necessary given the availability of logical and natural consequences. See the earlier classroom management suggestion on Consequences (Logical, Natural, *and* Contrived).

Let's assume, though, that you decide to go ahead and punish a student. The "qualifier for punishment" that I offer is that you understand that whatever you use as a punishment will likely bring about negative attitudes on the part of the student toward that punishment. This relationship between the punishment used and the student's attitude toward that punishment is often overlooked.

Take, for instance, the assigning of writing as punishment. Although a survey by Hogan (1985, p. 41) of 117 teachers revealed that "only 6% of the respondents at all levels approved of the practice," twenty-seven percent of the teachers indicated that it occurred "very frequently" or "frequently." Forty percent said it occurred "sometimes." Male teachers were more disapproving than female teachers, and elementary teachers were slightly more disapproving than middle and senior high teachers. It seems as if teachers USE this method of punishment far more often than they actually APPROVE of it.

The problem with writing as punishment, according to Chamberlin (1971, p. 314), is that it is "too easily borne and too ordinary to be efficient," reducing "the legitimate work of the schoolroom to disgraceful drudgery." When teachers use writing as punishment, they convey the attitude that, "By doing this I know this is the worst thing I can make you do because writing is a hateful activity and a kind of punishment" DeReign 1983, p. 79). Do we really want students to develop such an attitude toward writing? I think not.

If not a cognitive-type activity such as writing for punishment, what then? Some teachers, like drill sergeants in the military, assign physical activities as punishment. The title of an article by Baden (1981), "Running Laps for Multiple Misspellings," helps make my point. Teachers who use such punishment overlook the fact that it "could develop in some students a negative or ambivalent attitude about physical education" (Davidman and Davidman 1984, p. 169).

Although certainly an unfair stereotyping, I can picture the physical education teacher who feels less competent in writing, assigning writing as a punishment, and the English teacher who feels less competent physically, assigning physical activities as punishment. Both have selected what

THEY feel to be the most punishing consequence. Both disregard the possibility that such consequences can have deleterious instructional outcomes. If you choose to punish, don't make the same mistake.

By now, you may have noted a real problem with trying to supply a form of punishment, and at the same time trying to avoid having students develop negative attitudes toward that punishment. I am not sure that it is possible, within the law and within students' ever-growing rights, to select any punishment that will not also carry the danger of students developing unwanted negative attitudes toward that punishment.

R for Return Assignments and Tests Quickly

What does this have to do with classroom management? Educational psychologists suggest that learners will not continue to learn unless they receive "knowledge of results," or more appropriately, "knowledge of correct results." If learners are not "continuing to learn," due to lack of prompt corrective feedback from you, what are they doing? They may be inclined to misbehave. Let them know how they are doing; let them know right away. Create the conditions that enhance students' continued learning — give them prompt feedback.

Learners want to know how they are doing. Presumably, the many assignments and tests that we require students to take are designed to provide just this information — to us and to them. We want students to be prepared, to be ready, to complete this work. We are prone to "get on their case" if they are late in submitting required work. Are students not entitled to be equally disturbed when we delay returning their work? How will they show this discontent? How would you show it? Misbehaving seems a likely student response.

If we don't act in a fashion that "tells" students that we think our assignments and tests are important, then how can we expect students to take them seriously? Returning student work as quickly as possible and doing as accurate a job scoring it as you can send students the right message: this work is important. Failing to return the work on time or within a reasonable time sends an entirely different message — this work really wasn't that important anyhow. Students start to think to themselves that if this work which was submitted is not seen as being that important to the teacher, then how can any future work be that important. This attitude could lead to disinterested students — the basis for misbehavior.

Don't let this happen. Go out of your way to return student work quickly. Model, through your behavior, the same importance your words try to convey.

R for Rules and Procedures

According to Evertson et al. (1989, p. 19), "A rule identifies general expectations or standards for behavior." Rules may describe both acceptable behavior

("Students may talk during change of classes") as well as unacceptable behavior ("Students may not smoke in school"). Rules also may be general in nature ("Students must respect school property") or specific in nature ("Students may only go to their lockers before school begins and after school ends").

Gnagey (1975), in describing William Glasser's basic elements required in order to produce good discipline, offers the following advice concerning rules. One, students must know the school rules. The rules should be displayed in a prominent place or duplicated in sufficient quantity for all students.

Two, within reason, students ought to agree with the rules. One way to accomplish this is to take the time to point out the cause and effect relationship between each rule and its likely outcome. "In general . . . the nature of a forbidden act should be carefully explained . . . and the reasons for its prohibition made clear" (Bagley 1914, p. 135). Having the rule, "Students must walk through the halls," should *cause* students to arrive at their destination more safely. Point this out. Most students see the logic or the rationale of such rules—especially after likely outcomes are explored. Keep in mind that your obligation as a teacher only extends to explaining *why* the rule is rational. That does not guarantee that all students will agree with the rules. Some will not; they still must obey them.

Three, consider having students participate in rule making and, for that matter, rule changing. It never ceases to amaze me that when students, with some prompting, take part in forming school (classroom) rules, their rules are very similar to those the teacher would have formed, if she had formed them completely on her own. "Raising one's hand before speaking," or "walking between classes" emerge no matter the origin. The difference, though, in having students take part in forming the rules is the degree of ownership students experience by doing so. The rules are not just the school's rules, they are the students' rules, too. Because circumstances change, rules should be able to be changed. They should not be cast in stone.

However, students must realize that there are, at times, school-wide rules that must be accepted as they are. They generally are not open to the same rule making and rule changing that may apply to individual classroom rules. "No smoking is permitted on school property," or "any students missing school must have a signed note from a parent or guardian" stand as stated.

Finally, students should know what will happen to them if they break the rules. "If a student contemplates breaking the rules, he should know the price he will have to pay. If the price (consequence) is logically related to the misbehavior, better discipline will result" (Gnagey 1975, p. 31).

Jones and Jones (1986, p. 199) add to the discussion of rules by stressing that rules should be clearly stated (for example, avoid general statements such as "behave yourself at all times"), should be kept to the fewest number possible, and will be more effective if students "know that the rules are accepted by significant others such as their parents and peers." I would add teachers to the list of significant others.

Bagley (1914, p. 43) offers a concluding comment on rules that is as timely now as it was three-quarters of a century ago, "A cardinal rule of school management is to have few rules, and these very specific and relentlessly enforced." Doyle (1986, p. 412) stresses the importance of enforcing rules when he states, "Rules that are not *enforced* do not remain *in force* in the class." When students break a rule, the appropriate consequence should be supplied, "dispassionately and matter-of-factly" (Charles 1985, p. 136).

In contrast to rules, procedures more often apply "in a *specific* activity, and are usually directed at accomplishing something rather than prohibiting some behavior . . ." (Evertson et al. 1989, p. 19). What procedures must students follow in order to function effectively in a school environment and, thus, to learn?

Evertson et al. (1981, pp. 28–40) identify specific areas, along with suggestions, where elementary teachers may need to establish procedures: use of classroom space and facilities, use of other areas of the school, whole class activities and seatwork, reading groups and other small groups, beginning and ending the school day, handling interruptions and delays, and responding to fire drills. At the junior high level, students have more going-to-school skills and thus the teacher may concentrate upon maintaining, rather than upon introducing and explaining, procedures.

Common to both elementary and secondary teachers is the fact that less effective teachers who do not establish rules and procedures to handle classroom behavior, in particular inappropriate behavior, are forced to ignore it, to make up a rule or procedure on the spot, or to cope with the problem ad hoc (Evertson and Emmer 1982, p. 494). This can only lead to classroom management problems.

S for Secure Their Attention — First!

Before you start, get everyone's attention. Common sense? Apparently not for everyone. McDaniel (1986, p. 63) points out that "beginning teachers often make the mistake of trying to teach over the chatter of inattentive students." He states further that some teachers "assume that, if they begin the lesson (and there are *many* beginning points within each lesson), students will notice and quiet down." How long should you wait until students notice? Two minutes? Five minutes? What if some students never notice? Eventually you will, if any effective teaching is going to take place, need to secure their attention. Since you are going to demand their attention at some point, why not make that point BEFORE STARTING TO TEACH?

If a student does not hear what you have said, sure enough he will lean across the aisle or talk across the room trying to get the information he missed. You will see this as misbehavior, and we are off and running with a discipline problem that did not need to exist in the first place. What may happen instead is that the student will interrupt the class to ask for the missing information. You will get upset that he did not pay attention in the first place, maybe tell him so either verbally or nonverbally, and once again we are off and running with a possible discipline problem that did not need to exist. The examples are endless.

Practice different strategies for securing their attention. Some are rather straightforward. You could simply tell them: "Okay, let's begin. Put everything but your math book away. It is time to start the math lesson for today." Other common ways of securing students' attention might be simply to stand in front of the class and say nothing. Silence is often the "loudest" message. You could play a chord or two on the piano, blink the lights, ring a bell, cough, tap the pointer on the board, and so on. When using any of the nonverbal methods for securing attention, BE SURE to first teach them what those messages mean. Lights being turned off could mean a power failure; a cough could mean a lingering cold; a tap of a pointer stick could be a nervous habit.

Parr and Peterson (1985, p. 40) offer an interesting variation to getting students to focus upon the lesson at hand. They suggest you embed an assumption or presupposition in what you say to them. For example, "While you quiet down and get settled in your seat, open your text to page 50," or "I don't know which part of this chapter will interest you the most, but. . . ." The first statement assumes they will "quiet down and get settled." The second statement presupposes something "will" interest them in the chapter.

Secure their attention before proceeding with your lesson.

S for Surprise Them or "How Did You Know That?"

Go out of your way to learn things about your students—their work in other classes, efforts and accomplishments in sports, part-time job experiences, home life, scouts. Actually, this is not really very difficult, and even less time-consuming, to do. Just keep your eyes and ears open.

This is not an exercise in gossip gathering. It is an exercise in collecting information on students and their lives that you can surprise them with when they least expect it. At the beginning of class you say, "Mary, how is the slinging of hamburgers going at McDonalds?" or "Larry, that was an interesting collage you did in art class," or "Sam, what's this I hear about you earning another merit badge in scouts?" Don't dwell on any one item. That's not the point. Don't give the students time to think how you know what you know. Just "drop" the surprise information, and go on with your scheduled lesson.

The effects of your "delivering" this NICE information are several. It certainly conveys to your students that you are tuned into their lives beyond simply how they are doing in your class. It shows that you recognize other accomplishments of theirs whether it is winning an award, scoring a touchdown, OR simply being persistent enough to show up night after night slinging hamburgers at a local fast-food joint. This effort on your part cannot help but strengthen the relationship between you and your students. It cannot help but enhance your "Referent Power." (See the Chapter III article, "French and Raven's Social Bases of Power" for more information on Referent Power.)

But surprising students with information you have about their lives does something else. It keeps students "on their toes" a little more. It keeps them wondering how you seem to know so much about them. They start to think that if you know this NICE information about them, perhaps you are also in a position to know when they might try to get away with something—misbehave. The effect of delivering this information is that students begin to think that you have eyes and ears everywhere.

A local principal readily admits to dropping this NICE information on his students as well as on his teachers. While they like to receive evidence that the principal is tuned in to what they are doing, at the same time they, too, are sure he has eyes and ears everywhere. He doesn't, they just think so. But, their perception that he does is enough. The result is that students (and, at times, teachers) exhibit more self-discipline—the *very best* classroom management technique.

Take the time to establish your "eyes and ears everywhere" image. After it is established, it takes only an occasional demonstration to maintain that image. Do it; it works! It works really well.

T for Teams; An Important Aspect of Control Theory

Most educators are familiar with Maslow's "Hierarchy of Needs" (see the Chapter III article, "Maslow's Hierarchy.") William Glasser has a slightly different list of the needs that drive us all including, among others, to belong and love, to gain power, and to have fun (Glasser 1986, p. 23).

Glasser (1986, p. 70) points out that in too many classes "there is little sense of fun and belonging and, except for a few high achievers, little sense of power." The contrast between activities built around teams (for example, sports, music, and drama) and those found in many traditional classrooms (learning and competing as individuals) is pronounced. Is it

any wonder that discipline problems emerge in traditional classrooms—an environment where students' need fulfillment may be hampered?

Because team-oriented activities are so satisfying, students will work long and hard—for the good of the team, for the good of the production, for the good of the school. Team members learn their running plays, learn their songs, learn their lines. Team members are involved —pulling together. Spirit exists. Participants in team-

oriented activities "belong," "gain importance," and, from all observations, "have fun." They fulfill their needs *and* learn along the way.

Does a football coach have power over team members because he/she
determines who sits on the bench and who doesn't? Perhaps. Does a
choral director have power over choir members because he/she selects
soloists? Maybe. Does a drama coach have power over thespians because
he/she assigns the starring roles? Could be. For those who support a
reward/punishment model, the answer is clearly "Yes." Glasser has
another explanation. He believes that these coaches and directors have
power over team members because team members see their respective
team as a need-fulfilling structure that leads to their success. While
engaging in activities that are perceived to fulfill their needs, there is little
reason or motivation to misbehave. What would be the point?

Glasser believes that we should move to classrooms in which students
work together in small learning-teams. He points out that few people, even
successful adults, can feel important by themselves. They know they are
good at what they do. "But most of us feel important only as members of a
team" (Gough 1987, p. 659). Glasser's reasons for learning-teams are
(1986, pp. 75–76):

> Students can gain a sense of belonging by working together in
> learning-teams.
> Belonging provides the initial motivation for students to work. As
> they achieve academic success, students who had not worked
> previously begin to sense that KNOWLEDGE IS POWER and
> they want to work harder. It becomes pleasantly addictive.
> Stronger students find it fulfilling to help weaker ones because they
> want the power and friendship that go with a high-performing
> team.
> Weaker students find it is need-fulfilling to contribute as much as
> they can because whatever they can contribute helps. When
> they worked alone, a little effort got them nowhere. Yet, as
> need-driven human beings, they still sought power and
> recognition—hence the seeds of a discipline problem.
> Students need not depend only on the teacher. By fostering this
> attitude, both a need for power and a need for freedom are
> enhanced.
> Teams are free to demonstrate creativity in convincing teachers
> and other teams that they have learned the material.
> Teams will be changed by the teacher on a regular basis, so that
> all students will have a chance to be on a high-scoring team.

Glasser believes that working in teams has evolved because we have
needs that are met by such a structure. In a good team "we satisfy our
need for BELONGING . . . we satisfy our need for POWER because we
can do so much more than by ourselves . . . and when we work well
together, we learn more and it's more FUN" (Brandt 1988, p. 40). It
sounds so easy, but it is not. It will require "a lot of time and effort (for

teachers) to work out an effective team assignment, and anything less doesn't work" (Brandt 1988, p. 41).

The point made earlier, that KNOWLEDGE IS POWER, needs to be reiterated. "There is no power in superficial knowledge" (Glasser 1986, p. 72). Teachers know this is the case; students must at least suspect this is the case. But how do we convince students of this point? Telling them it is so, like we tell them so many other things are so, will not work. Working in learning-teams, while encouraging creative ways of demonstrating what they have learned, might just achieve this recognition.

Once the fact that KNOWLEDGE IS POWER is recognized, look out. Students will be driven (need-fulfillment) to gain still greater depths of knowledge. There simply will not be enough time and energy, nor will there be any reason, to misbehave.

T for Say "Thank You"

When students do something for you, say "Thank You" and mean it. If they have been cooperative, if they have done anything at all that has made your job even a little bit easier and more pleasant, show your appreciation. Thank them. Try saying "Thank you" when students turn in homework, head their paper correctly, carry something for you, pick something up off the floor, help another student (this also helps you), hold open a door for you, quietly take their place in line, get quickly into their reading groups, and so on. . . .

Why do they deserve your thanks for doing no more than what they should be doing anyhow? Well, for one thing, it is the polite thing to say. For another thing, thank you is said, especially to students and children, far too infrequently. Since no damage can be done by saying it, why not err on the side of saying it too often rather then not enough.

If you want to really catch students off guard (in a positive sense), say thank you (inferred to mean, "Thank You for all your time and effort you put into this exam") as they individually hand in tests or quizzes. If you think about it, most students taking the test have sat through your lectures, completed your assignments, read the chapters you have assigned, studied for your test, and now have just devoted an hour or so of their lives to taking your test. A thank you is in order. Without students, there would be no need for teachers. Besides, the thank you helps temper what may have otherwise been a pretty anxiety-ridden experience.

When possible, identify the specific behavior of theirs for which you are thanking them. This results in a cause-and-effect relationship between a deed and a thank you. At other times, such as when they have labored over your test, just a simple thank you without further explanation is sufficient.

Saying thank you lets them know you know they are there, they are being noticed, they are being appreciated. It shows them that they play a key role in helping to make the lives of those around them more pleasant. After all, we are all too ready to point out to them when they make our life unpleasant, aren't we? Saying thank you also models for students the appropriate way to respond when others make your life just a little bit easier. Who knows, students may end up saying thank you to you as well as to classmates. It really could happen.

Make a habit of saying thank you. Do it; it works!

P.S. By the way, thank you for taking the time and effort to read this book.

T for Threats and Warnings

Don't threaten to take action. Take action. If you have a discipline plan, then the plan dictates that either action IS WARRANTED or it IS NOT WARRANTED. There can be no other choice! Your discipline plan, the agreed-upon rules, should be clear enough to all concerned so that teachers and students alike understand what triggers the plan and what does not.

Threats can undermine an otherwise successful discipline plan. They make discipline personal, when it need not be—should not be. Even worse, some teachers use their threats AS their discipline plan—forming it "on the run." Students are forced to interpret and/or extrapolate from the threats just what the teacher's discipline plan is. Woe to the student who does not figure out the plan in time.

All that usually happens when teachers threaten is that students try to figure out just how far they can go before the teacher will actually carry out the threat. "When teachers finally decide to impose consequences, hostility and ill feelings are likely to result for everyone" (Charles 1985, p. 136). A discipline plan based or formed on a series of teacher threats is often heavily influenced by a teacher's feelings. If a teacher feels great one day, students can get away with more. If a teacher feels lousy another day, students can get away with less. Too much precious student time and energy are wasted playing this decoding game. Once again, woe to the student who misreads a teacher's feelings and goes too far that day.

Another trouble with threats is that, after a while, they are ineffective unless they are carried out. How many teachers have you heard threaten to throw kids out of class, threaten to suspend or expel them, threaten to "murder" them? Obviously, far more teachers are going to carry out their threat of "throwing a kid out of class" than will carry out their threat of "murdering" a student. Which threats are the students to believe? What happens to classroom discipline when threats are made and found to be unenforceable? Teachers should never paint themselves into a corner by promising (threatening) what they can't deliver!

Nothing is to be gained by threats. Avoid them. When tempted to threaten a student, refer to your thought-out discipline plan. Let it dictate your actions—not your threats!

Is there any place in a teacher's discipline plan for issuing warnings? Charles (1985, p. 137) feels that a warning should only be given once, if at all. Even that warning might take the form of the teacher's saying, "The next time you do such and such, I must enforce the consequence (penalty) you seem to be choosing."

U for Be Up

Wouldn't it be wonderful if the advice, "Don't worry; Be happy," displayed on millions of Smiley-faced t-shirts, could be followed? But reality often dictates otherwise. Reality or not, when you enter the school, try your best to leave your worries outside. They can be recovered after school when you leave. No one will take them.

Carrying personal problems into the classroom can interfere with your teaching and with students learning. Non-health-related problems such as insurance bills that are due, a fight with one's spouse, or a recent fender bender can put a real damper on one's day. I understand that. But you need to deal with these problems on your own time, not the students' time.

If a student says, "Good morning, Mrs. Knouse, how are you?" you don't have to lie and say, "I am doing tremendous." Besides, the emphasis you would place on these words and your accompanying body language would probably send a mixed message. You could just say, "Not bad, how about you?" Often these "How are you's," whether initiated by you, a student, or a fellow teacher, are just polite ways of acknowledging each other. While on the run, most people do not want to listen to your problems, anyhow. On the other hand, during a planning period when you and a valued friend or colleague have some private time, you might bend his or her ear for awhile. Once the bell rings, put the problem away and get on with devoting your full attention to being a teacher.

There are problems of a health nature that sometimes make them difficult to conceal. These cannot be placed on the school's doorstep. A sprained back after falling on the ice the night before that impedes your movement about the room can be a problem. If it is a problem, it probably ought to be shared, with as few details as possible, with students in order to let them know what to expect that day. For instance, "Due to a fall I had on the ice, I will not be able to come back to your desk when you raise your hand. Instead, I would like you to help me by coming up, one at a time, to my desk when you need assistance."

In general, do what the title of the suggestion says, "Be Up." It can be contagious, spreading throughout the school. What a wonderful epidemic it would be.

V for Visibility (and at Times Invisibility)

The bell has rung, and students are changing class. Where are you? The students are called for an assembly. Where are you? Numerous extracurricular events are taking place. Where are you? My suggestion is that you make yourself visible. Let students note your presence.

When classes are changing, consider standing near the doorway so that you can monitor both your room *and* the hallway outside of your room. Present the appearance that you are ready to deal with disciplinary infractions when you see them—in or out of your room. Keep in mind that, legally, any and all students in the school are partially your responsibility. Your responsibility for discipline is school-wide; it does not end with the last person on your homeroom or class roster.

Will the end result of being more visible be more discipline work for you? No! In fact, the more visible you (as well as fellow teachers) are, the less often students will misbehave. Misbehaving students are opportunistic. Let's don't give them quite so many opportunities. Drivers speed less often when the police are visible. Siblings often battle less when parents are visible. Students misbehave less when teachers are visible.

Now, what about being invisible? I recommend that you purchase a pair of soft-soled shoes that will enable you to move about the classroom, study hall, assembly, lunchroom, or building while making the minimum noise possible. Unlike police who turn on their sirens blocks away for all to hear, teachers should be able to move about without their noisy shoes providing advance notice. In addition to the fact that the noise may be annoying to students who *are* trying to work, it is a clear giveaway to students who *are not* working. Vary your path and time schedule so that you are not so predictable. "Good" students perceive that you are available, and "not-so-good" students think you are everywhere! (Graff 1981, p. 3)

Be visible—at the right times. Be invisible—at the right times.

V for Vocational/Technical School Experience

The Problem

Does this suggestion have a bearing on classroom management? You decide. In Pennsylvania, for instance, 168,500 students take part in vocational/technical programs yearly. This represents forty-one percent of all tenth through twelfth grade students in the Commonwealth. More than 60,000 of these students attend eighty-five area vocational/technical schools (AVTS) on some sort of split schedule—for example, one week at the home academic school and one week at the AVTS.

Just how prepared is the average secondary classroom teacher to teach vo/tech-oriented students the English, mathematics, social studies, and science they require? Through no fault of their own, the answer is, "These teachers are not at all well prepared." Typical middle-class, college-educated teachers are ones who, themselves, have come out of a college preparatory program while in high school. That's what they understand. That is where their empathies often lie.

It is not uncommon for academically oriented students to refer to vo/tech students as "tech rats," "votards," and "spleds," while their teachers dread when it is their turn to HAVE TO TEACH the vo/tech students. The theory behind the self-fulfilling prophecy (see the Chapter III article, "Self-Fulfilling Prophecy") tells us that these negative expectations on the part of both teachers and peers will set into motion a process that is almost guaranteed to cause problems. Often these problems surface in the form of classroom management difficulties. Surely, with these dynamics in place, the occurrence of discipline problems should come as no surprise.

To add a little fuel to the fire, states often require vo/tech students to take the same minimum number of credits in key academic areas as non-vo/tech students. For students attending an AVTS, this results in their having to double up on academic subjects during their week at the home academic school—two periods a day of English, social studies, and so on.

The Solution

The solution to many of the discipline problems that exist in classrooms of vo/tech students, from general lack of motivation to outright rebellious behavior, partially lies in educators not learning more about vo/tech schools and programs. It is here where a large percentage of their students will spend up to one-half of their school hours. If we want students to be interested in our areas (subjects), then we simply must demonstrate an informed interest in their areas.

For those schools that offer in-house vo/tech programs (for example, Distributive Education, Agriculture Education), an academic teacher can take the time and make the effort to visit these shops, see what happens there, talk (and maybe plan) with shop instructors, and, where possible, incorporate what has been learned in class assignments, lectures, and discussions.

For those high schools where students attend an AVTS, educators (teachers and administrators) must take the extra time and make the extra effort to visit, explore, *and* possibly, sample what these schools have to offer. AVTSs are really just an extension of vo/tech students' academic high school. Instead of the shop's being down the hall or in the school's basement, it just happens to be located in a separate building several miles away.

Try sampling what a vo/tech school has to offer. Pull your hair back, put on some work clothes, step into their world, and try it for a day. Be the novice. Let a vo/tech student be your tutor. Select a shop that is rather far removed from your experience—for example, tool and die, metal fabrication. You will survive! How do I know? Well, over the past decade I have worked with many teachers, just like you, who have taken part in just such an experience (Tauber 1978).

If possible, work out an arrangement with your principal whereby you can take part in just the kind of hands-on experience described above. Participating teachers come away with a much better understanding of the vo/tech world—its goals and its methods. More importantly, participants gain a new respect for what, until this experience, has been a foreign world. Participants come away amazed at the pride students take in their work, the attention paid to detail, the unsupervised cafeteria, the extensive technical library, the use of students as foremen or office managers, the heavy reliance on mathematics, and on and on.

Often discipline problems are caused when a student tries to play one end against the other. In a broken home a child can tell one parent one thing and the other parent something else. As long as the two parents do not communicate, the child has the upper hand. So, too, it is with students who spend part of their time in an AVTS and the other part in the home high school. The kind of experience I have described increases communication between the home school teacher and the AVTS instructor.

If you can't work out release time to participate in such an experience, at least try taking part in one of the many adult evening programs offered at your nearby vo/tech school. Once again, select a program that is very different from your experiential base. The cost of the experience will be minimal. The payoff will be lifelong.

For the record, *elementary teachers have just as much of a reason to take part in a vo/tech hands-on experience as do secondary teachers.* Just think of the motivational, let alone career awareness, opportunities such an experience could open up for your youngsters. And more to the point of this book, motivated students have less need to misbehave.

W for Wait-Time

An analysis of teachers questioning behavior shows that it is not at all uncommon for them to wait no more than a second before repeating a question, rephrasing it, or calling upon someone else (Rowe 1978, p. 207). Further, according to Rowe (p. 207), "Once a student has responded, the teacher typically waits less than one second . . . before commenting on the answer or asking another question."

The net result of this pattern of behavior often is a flurry of questions and answers that leaves, at best, both the teacher and the student exhausted, and, at worst, does little "to stimulate a student's thought or quality of explanation" (Rowe 1978, p. 207). According to Rowe, when teachers extended their wait-time to three seconds or more, several things happened. The length of student responses increased, the number of unsolicited but appropriate responses increased, failures to respond decreased, incidences of speculative thinking increased, contributions by slow learners increased, *and,* related to the focus of this book, *the number of disciplinary moves the teachers had to make dropped dramatically!*

The anticipated increase in discipline problems due to the teacher's not keeping "the action going" simply did not materialize. Students did not use this three-second wait-time to act up; they used it to think. Tobin and Capie (1982) support this conclusion in a study that showed a significant positive correlation between wait-time and achievement. The message here is that a better way to maintain classroom discipline (as well as to increase learning) is to keep the students busy THINKING, not necessarily ANSWERING rapid-paced questions so common in many of today's classrooms.

W for Use **W**e, Not You

We are all in this together with a shared responsibility for the success or failure of today's class, this semester, the school year. A behavioral problem is not just a student's problem, nor is it just a teacher's problem. It is a problem for both. In order to increase *our* chances of success and reduce *our* chances of failure, cooperation is the name of the game. Preach this message; practice this message. The more the idea of shared responsibility and mutual cooperation is accepted, the less likely there will be behavioral problems.

Consider the hidden message delivered in the following statements — both designed to set the stage for the morning's activities. "This morning *we* are going to complete *our* science write-up during the first half of *our* morning, and then *we* will use the remaining time to discuss the selection of books *you and I* think *we* should request the library to order." "This morning *you* are going to complete *your* science write-up during the first half of the (*your*) period, and then *you* can use the remaining time to discuss the selection of books (*you think*) the library should order."

The first statement contains a lot of mutual ownership — our write-up, our morning, our discussion, our request. It conveys a message that the teacher will be working just as hard as the students. In fact, this is what will normally occur. The students set about doing the write-up while the teacher circulates among them answering some questions and asking still others, making comments, offering words of encouragement, posing what-if situations, and more. Such assignments are no free ride for a teacher. The *we* in the message suggests that the teacher is asking no more of his or her students than he or she is willing to do. Both are working. It is clear that the teacher and students are in this together.

In the second statement there is little, if any, mutual ownership. It appears that only the students have work to do; only they will work to complete the assignments. The teacher's role seems to be one of simply telling students what they will do (for example, "you are going to . . ."). I wonder what the teacher will be doing? "You do this," and "you do that" statements from teachers are often accompanied by finger pointing. Have you ever tried to point your finger at someone and say "we"? It is like trying to shake your head back and forth and say "yes" at the same time.

What is done in a classroom usually involves both the teacher and the student. Together they can make quite a team. Together they can complete assignments, make plans, solve problems, and so on. Where it applies, use "we" rather than "you" when talking with students.

X for Exemplify Desired Behavior; Don't Be a Hypocrite

Most of us have been in the position where someone in authority has said, "Don't do as I do, do as I say." Try to remember how you felt when he/she made that statement. Think of how you felt when the person used that authority to enforce his/her demand. You probably felt some resentment. You probably thought to yourself, "Where do you get off telling me to do such and such? You do it all the time—you hypocrite." The bottom line is for educators to practice what they preach.

Although there are legitimate times when, as an adult and as a teacher, you will have the right to do things your students are not permitted to do, such instances should be kept to a minimum. RHIP (Rank Has Its Privileges), though steeped in fraternity, military, and societal tradition, can cause discipline problems if abused. When you do things that students are not permitted to do, especially if you flaunt it, it offends their sense of fairness. Children see fairness in simple black-and-white terms. Although maturity helps clarify their view of fairness, until they achieve maturity, what is good for the goose is seen as good for the gander, as far as they are concerned.

I understand that you have worked long and hard to become a teacher— a respected professional in the community. Shouldn't certain privileges accompany the title? Haven't you earned the right to do all the things you saw many of your teachers doing when you were a student? Although the answer may be "yes," from a classroom management viewpoint it would be best to control the temptation to do so.

Try to put yourself back into the position of a student. Try to look at your behavior through their eyes. What do you suppose they are thinking when, during your thirty-minute, duty-free lunch period, you cut into the lunch line? Are you really any more hungry than the students? Even if you are, does that give you the right to cut in? When you constantly interrupt students when they are speaking and yet criticize them when they do so, where is the fairness? When you tell them that you just bought a radar detector, is it fair in the same breath to chastise them for cheating on a test or for plagiarizing a term paper? After all, what is the radar detector used for other than to cheat on the speed limit—the law? Your actions do speak louder than your words.

Keep in mind that students learn a lot more from observing models or exemplars (for example, teachers) than may be readily evident in their observed performance. The learning has taken place even if students are reluctant to repeat the observed behavior. Study after study has shown that, when enticed (perhaps by peers or by other circumstances) to demonstrate an earlier observed behavior, *most students* are capable of repeating that behavior. Watch what you are doing; others are. Don't let your words and actions make you a hypocrite. Exemplify desired behaviors.

Y for Don't Ask **Why**

No matter how very tempting it is do so, don't ask a student "Why" he misbehaved! It leads nowhere, except to problems. All people, including children, like to believe that they do things for a reason. They want to perceive themselves as rational human beings. In fact, we like to think of others around us as acting in rational vs. irrational ways. The world would just be too scary if people did not act rationally.

When you ask a student why he did what he did (for example, hit Cissie, threw a pencil at Bobby, didn't complete the homework), he feels bound to give you an answer — a reason that would justify his actions. He wants to appear rationale. He says he hit Cissie because she hit him first. He threw the pencil because Bobby called him names. He didn't complete the homework because he had swimming lessons at the YMCA. I can guarantee that the student WILL HAVE an answer that, at least to him, sounds rational. Unfortunately, the reasons never seem to be good enough to appease teachers. They simply will not buy what they think are the students' "excuses."

Teachers will respond by saying that just because Cissie hit him is no reason to hit her; Bobby calling him names is not a justification for throwing a pencil at him; having swimming lessons is no excuse for incomplete homework. One wonders, then, *why teachers bother to ask "Why" when they rarely, if ever, accept the reasons offered.*

Soon students learn not to give their reasons even if asked to do so. Why bother? The teacher will not believe them anyhow. Instead, they try the "I don't know" response. How do teachers, in turn, respond to this tactic? They say, "What do you mean, you don't know; of course you know, now tell me!" So, the student blurts out HIS reason, HIS rationale, only, once again, not to have the "excuse" accepted.

A third student response, actually a nonverbal version of the second response, may finally appear. Here the student being asked his reasons for what he did, simply stands there, looks down at the floor, and shrugs his shoulders conveying nonverbally, "I don't know why I did it, I just did." But, as was the case with the first two responses to the teacher's question of "Why?," the teacher is not willing to accept shrugged shoulders. Who knows, maybe with younger children a little bit of shaking those shoulders will elicit a verbal response. What the use of this would be I don't know because even if a verbal response is shaken loose, it will be no more acceptable to teachers than the nonverbal response.

The message here is to avoid dwelling on the past — that is part of your world and the child's world that cannot be changed. Instead, one needs to concentrate on the present *and* on the future. One needs to take appropriate measures that will stop (or, more realistically, significantly reduce) hitting fellow students, throwing pencils across the room, and not turning in assigned homework.

It is okay for a teacher, according to Glasser's reality therapy, to ask a child WHAT he did. This question helps make sure that both the teacher and the student are focusing upon the same student behavior; it helps students take the responsibility for "owning up" to wrong doings; and it sets the stage for Glasser's suggestion that students (not teachers) be asked to come up with a plan that will see to it that the misbehavior will not happen in the future. Asking a child WHAT he did is very, very different from asking him WHY he did what he did.

Go ahead, ask the WHAT question; it works! Avoid asking the WHY question; it does not work! See the Chapter III article, "Glasser's Reality Therapy."

Z for **Z**ap Solution Messages

The stronger the teacher/student relationship, the less need for classroom management techniques. One situation that can undermine this relationship is how a teacher responds when a student owns a problem— often one where strong feelings and emotions are involved. For instance, a student may feel defeated because he did not score well on his SAT exams or may be sad over a good friend's moving away. These situations, and thousands more, *can* become discipline (as well as academic) problems if the feelings that accompany the situations persist and thus interfere with a student's schoolwork.

In the situations described above, it is the student who owns the problem. As a helping agent we must, of course, show empathy. According to Gordon (1974), we must also feel reasonably separated from the problem, *and* we must believe that the student is the person best capable of either solving the problem or at least handling the strong feelings that accompany the problem.

A frequent teacher response to a student who owns a problem is to offer him suggestions or solutions. Although well-intended, sending a solution hinders the student's solving his problem, puts a strain on the teacher/student relationship, and sets the stage for possible discipline problems. Let's examine why sending a solution may be an inappropriate teacher response when a student owns a problem.

How does a student feel when you provide him with a workable solution to his problem? Initially, the feeling is one of gratefulness and appreciation. His problem is solved; a weight has been lifted from his shoulders. A little later, though, many students think, "Gee, I could have thought of that solution." In fact, in most cases students could have thought of your solution, or perhaps even a better one of their own, *if only they had been given the opportunity.*

What message is sent, between the lines, along with your well-intended solution? Could it be that you lack faith in the student's ability to come up with a solution? Even if your lack of faith is justified, just when will the student ever learn to solve problems if solutions are always handed to him? Handing out solutions, no matter how good they are (in your mind), suggests superiority on your part, and has as the end result of making the student dependent upon the solution giver—you. What will he do next time when you are not there? Could his inability to solve future problems lead to discipline problems?

Providing solutions helps a student duck responsibility. A student is less likely to assume responsibility for executing a solution that was not his in the first place. If a student follows YOUR solution and YOUR solution fails, then who is to blame? One guess—YOU—it was YOUR solution, wasn't it?

Some teachers find themselves defending THEIR solutions. The situation goes like this. You offer a solution. A student offers his reasons why he does not think your solution will work. You, in turn, feel a need to defend, justify, or sell your volunteered solution. This leads nowhere except to hard feelings on both sides.

Prefacing your solution with the statement, "Now you don't have to follow my advice, but, if I were you, I would do such and such . . . ," overlooks the status that teachers have in a student's eyes—especially an elementary student. A student feels he must, in fact, follow advice given by a teacher. Although this may be true in the academic world where the teacher may know best, it does not follow that the teacher knows best in the personal trials and tribulations faced by students.

Finally, and perhaps the most strange sounding of all, is Gordon's (1974) caution to think twice before giving advice or solutions, even when specifically asked to do so. Students who pour out their problem and end with a direct question, such as, "What would you do in my situation?" or "What do you think I should do?" really do not want your solution. These questions are simply an awkward way of turning the conversation over to you for a moment while the student decides whether to talk more about his problem. Even if asked, don't fall into the trap of giving students your two cents' worth of advice. It is so tempting to do so.

How can you be of help if you do not offer solutions? Actually, the act of *not offering* solutions is, in and of itself, a help. If you want to do still more, try decoding and then feeding back the feelings surrounding the problem that you think the student is experiencing. "The low SAT scores really have you depressed, huh?" "It's pretty sad to have a good friend move away, right?" Each attempt to reflect the student's feelings should provide the student with the opportunity to affirm or disaffirm the accuracy of your response. The student remains in control of the conversation.

Keep in mind that you can't change the low SAT scores, nor can you bring the student's best friend back. The student must learn to deal with the debilitating feelings surrounding his problems. Helping him to recognize these feelings goes a long way toward helping him deal with them. No solution message can do this.

How do you respond to direct appeals for advice? Try saying, "It seems as though you really are undecided about what to do," or "It sounds as if you are having a tough time deciding what your next step will be." If really pressed for YOUR solution, simply say that you feel you are not in any position to give such advice but that you would be glad to continue playing role of listener. Let's ZAP solution messages.

See the Chapter III article, "Gordon's Teacher (Parent) Effectiveness Training" for more information on active listening, a preferred way of responding.

REFERENCES

Baden, R. (1981). Running laps for multiple misspellings. *Media and Methods, 17*(5), 20–21. EJ 240-196.

Bagley, W. (1914). *School discipline.* New York: The Macmillan Company.

Balson, M. (1982). *Understanding classroom behaviour.* Hawthorne, Victoria: The Australian Council for Educational Research Limited.

Bartosh, F., Jr., & Barilla, J. (1985). Discipline — Still number one on the administrator's list of problems. *NASSP Bulletin, 69*(479), 6–10. EJ 315-236.

Brandt, R. (1988). On students' needs and team learning: A conversation with William Glasser. *Educational Leadership 45*(6), 38–45. EJ 370-222.

Britton, P., & Stallings, J. (1981). Changing a climate — Weary warriors to hardy hunters. *NASSP Bulletin, 65*(441), 58–64. EJ 238-674.

Burns, J. (1985). Discipline: Why does it continue to be a problem? Solution is in changing school culture. *NASSP Bulletin, 69*(479), 1–5. EJ 315-235.

Canter, C., & Canter, M. (1976). *Assertive discipline.* Seal Beach, CA: Canter and Associates.

Chamberlin, L. (1971). *Effective instruction through dynamic discipline.* Columbus, OH: Merrill.

Charles, C. (1985). *Building classroom discipline.* New York: Longman Inc.

Davidman, L., & Davidman, P. (1984). Logical assertion: A rationale and strategy. *The Educational Forum, 48*(2), 165–176. EJ 299-119.

DeReign, V. (1983). An English teacher's lament or what's wrong with writing as punishment. *English Journal, 72*(2), 79. No EJ number cited.

Dinkmeyer, D., & Dreikurs, R. (1963). *Encouraging children to learn.* Englewood Cliffs, NJ: Prentice-Hall, Inc.

Doyle, W. (1986). Classroom organization and management. In M. Wittrock (Ed.), *Handbook of research on teaching* (Chapter 14). New York: Macmillan Publishing Co.

Erikson, E. (1963). *Childhood and society.* New York: Norton. (First edition published in 1950.)

Evertson, C., & Emmer, E. (1982). Effective management at the beginning of the school year in junior high classes. *Journal of Educational Psychology, 74*(4), 485–498. EJ 267-792.

Evertson, C. et al. (1989). *Classroom management for elementary teachers.* Englewood Cliffs, NJ: Prentice-Hall.

Evertson, C. et al. (1981). *Organizing and managing the elementary school classroom.* Austin, TX: The University of Texas.

Glasser, W. (1986). *Control theory in the classroom.* New York: Harper & Row, Publishers.

Gnagey, W. (1975). *Maintaining discipline in classroom instruction.* New York: Macmillan Publishing Co., Inc.

Gordon, T. (1974). *Teacher effectiveness training.* New York: Peter H. Wyden, Inc.

Gough, P. (1987). The key to improving schools: An interview with William Glasser. *Phi Delta Kappan, 68*(9), 656–662. EJ 352-313.

Graff, P. (1981). Student discipline—Is there a bag of tricks? Or is organization the solution? *NASSP Bulletin, 65*(441), 1–5. EJ 238-662.

Hogan, M. (1985). Writing as punishment. *English Journal, 74*(5), 40–42. EJ 320-916.

Hyman, I., & D'Alessandro, J. (1984). Good, old-fashioned discipline: The politics of punitiveness. *Phi Delta Kappan, 66*(1), 39–45. EJ 306-689.

Jones, V., & Jones, L. (1986). *Comprehensive classroom management.* Boston: Allyn and Bacon, Inc.

Kounin, J. (1970). *Discipline and group management.* New York: Holt, Rinehart, & Winston, Inc.

Lasley, T. (1981). Helping teachers who have problems with discipline—A model and instrument. *NASSP Bulletin, 65*(441), 6–15. EJ 238-663.

Lewis, R., & Lovegrove, M. (1984). Teachers' classroom control procedures: Are students' preferences being met? *Journal of Research for Teaching, 10*(2), 97–105. EJ 300-690.

Mager, R. (1968). *Developing attitude toward learning.* Palo Alto, CA: Fearon Publishers.

McDaniel, T. (1986). A primer on classroom discipline: Principles old and new. *Phi Delta Kappan, 68*(1), 63–67. EJ 341-137.

Mendler, A., & Curwin, R. (1983). *Taking charge in the classroom.* Reston, VA: Reston Publishing Company, Inc.

Morgan, K. (1984). Calm discipline. *Phi Delta Kappan, 66*(1), 53–54. EJ 306-692.

National Education Association (1987). Today's Children: A Profile. *Today's Education, 5*(1), 23.

Palonsky, S. (1977). Teacher effectiveness in secondary schools: An ethnographic approach. *High School Journal, 41*(2), 45–51. EJ 174-990.

Parr, G., & Peterson, A. (1985). Friendly persuasion. *The Science Teacher, 52*(1), 39–40. EJ 312-679.

Rowe, M. (1978). Wait, wait, wait. . . . *School Science and Mathematics, 68*(685), 207–216. EJ 180-032.

Shrigley, R. (1985). Curbing student disruption in the classroom: Teachers need intervention skills. *NASSP Bulletin, 69*(479), 26–32. EJ 315-239.

Soltz, V. (1967). *Study group leader's manual.* Chicago: Alfred Adler Institute.

Stefanich, G., & Bell, L. (1985). A dynamic model of classroom discipline. *NASSP Bulletin, 69*(479), 19–25. EJ 315-238.

Tauber, R. (1978). Turning academic educators on to voc ed. *American Vocational Journal, 53*(3), 53–55. EJ 178-830.

Tauber, R. (1988). Overcoming misunderstanding about the concept of negative reinforcement. *Teaching of Psychology, 15*(3), 152–153. No EJ number yet assigned.

Tenoschok, M. (1985). Handling discipline problems. *Journal of Physical Education, Recreation and Dance, 56*(2), 29–30. EJ 314-601.

Tobin, K., & Capie, W. (1982). The relationship between classroom process variables and middle-school science achievement. *Journal of Educational Psychology, 74*(3), 441–454. EJ 265-354.

Weiten, W. (1989). *Psychology: Themes and variations.* Pacific Grove, CA: Brooks/Cole Publishing Company.

Wolfgang, C., & Glickman, C. (1980). *Solving discipline problems.* Boston: Allyn and Bacon, Inc.

Wolfgang, C., & Glickman, C. (1986). *Solving discipline problems.* Boston: Allyn and Bacon, Inc.

Note: The EJ number (for example, EJ 306-689) that follows each journal article can be used, in conjunction with the ERIC system described in Chapter IV, to obtain a copy of that article.

Selected Articles on Aspects of Classroom Management

The following short articles, specifically identified below, present ideas and skills that may have been under-presented, incorrectly presented, or overlooked completely in prior course work. An understanding of one's power bases, how one might successfully defuse power struggles, the confusion over negative reinforcement, the value of Gordon's I-Messages, to name just a few, is necessary in order to establish and maintain classroom discipline.

FRENCH AND RAVEN'S
SOCIAL BASES OF POWER
Reward, Coercive, Legitimate, Referent, Expert

INTRODUCTION

A school is a study in group dynamics, a study of how a teacher exerts power or influence over students, and how a principal exerts influence over faculty, staff, and students.

More than twenty-five years ago, French and Raven (1960) identified five specific bases of social power that can be used by educators to influence students. These five bases are coercive, reward, referent, legitimate, and expert power.

OVERUSED AND INEFFECTIVELY USED POWER SOURCES

From the 1950s through the early 1970s, the influence of behavior modification proponents prompted an overuse of both coercive and reward powers. Actually, such carrot-and-stick techniques had been used by educators for centuries. The new trend was an attempt to develop these practices into a scientific theory.

Coercive Power

Because students recognize the teacher's right and ability to mediate punishment, students allow teachers to influence them. But how much is really known about the effects of punishment on behavior? How many educators know how effectively to use punishment as a basis for social power and influence? How many know the limitations of punishment, especially on the relationship between the teacher and student? How many are deceived by the immediate, although short-lasting, effects of punishments?

Students cope with repeated punishment in a variety of ways. We have all seen coping techniques that range from rebelling, retaliating (if not at the teacher, then at a weaker classmate), lying, and cheating, to conforming, apple polishing, submitting, and withdrawing (either mentally or physically) from learning. Gordon (1974), however, states that these coping mechanisms are only visible signs of the student's anger, frustration, embarrassment, feelings of unworthiness, fear, humility, and vindictiveness. Clearly, knowing just a little bit about punishment does little good.

I am not suggesting that teachers avoid using coercive power. However, if they continue to rely on coercive power, they have a responsibility to learn enough about it to use it effectively.

Reward Power

Reward power allows teachers to exert influence because students recognize the teacher's ability to dole out rewards. Reward power is referred to by various names such as contingency management, shaping, operant conditioning, and token economies, and is surrounded by a vocabulary that includes words like stimulus, response, behavior, consequence, variable/fixed/ratio/interval, and reinforcement.

Unfortunately, familiarity with the vocabulary does not guarantee that educators will be able to use the theory. Without an understanding of the concept and the confidence that accompanies understanding, teachers too often react to discipline crises with only bits and pieces of operant learning theory and then wonder why the theory does not work.

For example, negative reinforcement is one of the four possible consequences to a student's behavior in the realm of reward power. (The other three consequences are positive reinforcement, punishment, and time-out.) How well do you and your colleagues understand negative reinforcement? Ask yourselves:

- What is another word for negative reinforcement? Many people answer punishment, yet this is not true — hence a misunderstanding.
- Would you use negative reinforcement to increase or decrease the chance of a behavior's occurring in the future? Many would answer "decrease," when in fact, the answer should be "increase."
- Do you believe students look forward to negative reinforcement? Many will answer "no" when, in fact, the answer is overwhelmingly "yes."
- Can you create an actual example of where you have purposely used negative reinforcement in your classroom? Usually the answer will be incorrect, or there will be no answer at all.

If teachers choose to exert reward power over students, they must use it effectively. If negative reinforcement is not understood, one of the four possible consequences to a student's behavior is eliminated as a tool of influence by the teacher. I suspect that educators do not understand the remaining consequences any better than they understand negative reinforcement.

OVERLOOKED BASES OF SOCIAL POWER AND INFLUENCE

As children move into their adolescent years, adults no longer possess either the physical or psychological control over the dissemination of rewards and punishment. What happens to those educators who have relied solely on coercive and reward power? As the child grows older, this power is less and less influential. Replacement sources of power and influence are needed. The ideal situation would be for the teacher to use all five of French and Raven's social bases of power all along. Then coercive and reward powers could be discarded when they are no longer effective.

Each of French and Raven's remaining sources of social power (legitimate, referent, and expert) have a far greater capacity to influence students than do coercive and reward power. Yet, for some reason they have been overlooked by both teachers and administrators who wish to do something about the discipline problem.

Legitimate Power

Students perceive that the teacher has the right to prescribe behavior. The students respect the teacher's social position or office. Legitimate power operates on the basis that people accept the social structure of institutions, including schools.

Inherent in this structure is a hierarchy of power. This power base is overlooked as a disciplinary method because we take it for granted that the students automatically respect teachers. After all, our society offers many examples for legitimate power. Preachers have the right to preach, and judges have the right to judge. However, the time is past when we can take it for granted that student respect for teachers is automatic. We must take some action to bring it about.

In their book, *Assertive Discipline,* Canter and Canter (1976) emphasize that teachers should recognize their legitimate power and use it to assert a high-profile, leadership role in the classroom. They suggest that the teacher should remind students that he or she has been assigned by the school board to lead the class and has been delegated the responsibility for seeing that conditions for learning are present. The teacher could make a statement such as, "I have a contract with the district to teach. I have an obligation to live up to the terms of that contract. Any disciplinary infractions that interfere with my efforts to teach and the efforts of other students to learn, cannot be tolerated."

Administrators could assist teachers by carrying this message of legitimate power throughout the building. They could stress in all their contacts with both school personnel and community members that within the social structure, teachers have been delegated the legitimate power to do what is necessary to keep the "learning act afloat."

When coercive power or reward power are used in conjunction with legitimate power, the result is much more effective. Thus, the benefits of legitimate power go beyond a single influence technique.

Referent Power

In cases of referent power, students identify with the teacher. They respect and are attracted to the teacher personally. The greater the attraction, the broader the range of referent power.

For instance, a math teacher may have referent power within the math classroom, and, because of the strong attraction the students feel for the teacher, the teacher is able to exert influence over the students outside the classroom — at a pep rally, in the cafeteria, while changing classes, and so on.

What creates this attraction, this oneness? Those teachers who possess referent power care about their students, and they show it in their actions. They are fair in their dealings with students, sacrificing neither their own convictions nor the students' legitimate rights. They do not solve problems for students, but instead respect the students enough to take the posture of facilitator, leaving the responsibility for change with the students. They communicate with students without seeing communication as a sign of weakness.

Teachers need assistance in developing their referent power. Thomas Gordon's (1974) *Teacher Effectiveness Training,* also available as *Leader Effectiveness Training* (1977) for administrators, is a good place to start. Gordon's communication model combines the theory and the practice with concrete skills for teachers to act as facilitators in the problem-solving process, to confront students and influence them willingly to modify their behavior, to substitute a no-lose for a win-lose conflict resolution technique, and more.

Learn about Dinkmeyer and Dinkmeyer's (1976) logical and natural consequences. Here, students see that certain consequences flow from their actions and not from the whim of the teacher or administrator. They see that discipline is fair.

Still more work could be done with Glasser's *Reality Therapy* (1969) and his ten steps to good discipline. Assuming, as Glasser does, that school must be seen as a good place, discipline can be achieved through a series of steps. These steps include not dwelling on why the offense occurred (all you will hear are excuses anyhow); asking the student to make a value judgment about his or her behavior (does it help the student, others, or for that matter, the world?); encouraging the student to make a plan to correct his or her behavior; and not administering any punishment.

Glasser observes that educators seem to have greater faith in disciplinary techniques that don't work — such as punishment. Rather than look for new techniques or ways to make present techniques more effective, educators simply continue using what in the past has not been successful.

Expert Power

Finally, we come to French and Raven's expert power, in which students perceive that teachers have special knowledge or expertise. They respect the teacher professionally. This source of power and influence is not consciously used because we expect students to recognize our expertness. But how can they when we don't recognize each other's expertise?

If you ask faculty members to identify the specific academic preparation of their peers, few can, to any great extent. Does this mean that they do not realize the breadth and depth of the expertness of their colleagues? I think so. Without this recognition, can they gain the shared strength and confidence from being part of a top-notch team? I don't think so.

Take this a little further. Quiz your own administration, school board, and parent advisory committees to see just how much they know about the strong academic preparation of the faculty. If these people "fail" the quiz, to what extent would you expect them to support you and your colleagues?

How will all of this affect teachers? Even the most basic understanding of Rosenthal and Jacobson's (1968) self-fulfilling prophecy reveals how the expectations of peers, administrators, board members, clients, and parents can have a definite effect on teachers to the extent that they will live up to or fulfill these expectations.

Imagine the effect on students if efforts were made school-wide and community-wide to illuminate the expertness of the faculty. The students would come into class expecting more from these "expert" teachers. These higher expectations of the students, as well as those of all others with whom the teachers come in contact, can cause the teachers to live up to these expectations. The more they live up to these expectations of expertness, the more they are perceived as experts, and thus the more of French and Raven's expert power and influence they possess.

To illuminate the expertness of one's professional staff, simply give credit to what is fact. At a minimum, this is deserved. Ask yourself what you have done lately to promote the expertness of your faculty legitimately. If you have not done much, think of what you can do, and then do it. The payoff to you is that teachers will then have another social base of power to improve discipline both within the classroom and throughout the school.

SUMMARY

If you accept French and Raven's argument for five social bases of power and influence, then you really can't afford to ignore any of the five. See that teachers are prepared to use all five effectively, to not overuse some, and to not overlook the others.

REFERENCES

Canter, L., & Canter, M. (1976). *Assertive discipline.* Seal Beach, CA: Canter and Associates.

Dinkmeyer, D., & Dinkmeyer, D., Jr. (1976). Logical consequences: A key to the reduction of disciplinary problems. *Phi Delta Kappan, 57*(10), 665–666. EJ 139–345.

French, J., Jr., & Raven, B. (1960). The bases for social power. D. Cartwright & J. Zander (Eds.), *Group dynamics: Research and theory,* Evanston, IL: Row-Peterson.

Glasser, W. (1969). *Schools without failure.* New York: Harper & Row.

See the Chapter III article entitled "Glasser's Reality Therapy," for
more information.

Gordon, T. (1974). *Teacher effectiveness training.* New York: Peter H.
Wyden; also *Leader effectiveness training.* (1977). New York: Bantam
Books, Inc.

Rosenthal, R., & Jacobson, L. (1968). *Pygmalion in the classroom.* New
York: Holt, Rinehart and Winston, Inc. An excellent summary of this
research is presented in Insel, P., & Jacobson, L. (1975). *What do you
expect? An inquiry into self-fulfilling prophecies.* Menlo Park, CA:
Cummings Publishing Co.

Note: The EJ number (for example, EJ 306–689) that follows each journal article can be
used, in conjunction with the ERIC system described in Chapter IV, to obtain a
copy of that article.

DEFUSING POWER STRUGGLES
Alternatives to "Fighting Back" or "Giving In"

INTRODUCTION

One of the most time-consuming and unrewarding duties of an educator is having to deal with discipline problems. Teachers can become more
effective disciplinarians by identifying the general categories of misbehavior, singling out one or more especially troublesome categories, recognizing ineffective ways of responding, and learning alternative methods.
Power struggles between teachers and students is one of those especially
troublesome categories of misbehavior. Teachers must learn how to
defuse power struggles effectively.

GOALS OF MISBEHAVIOR

There are four goals of misbehavior (Dreikurs, Grunwald, and Pepper
1971). They are attention, power, revenge, and display of inadequacy.
These goals form a hierarchy that reflects the degree of discouragement
felt by the student. Attention, at the top of the hierarchy, represents mild
discouragement. Display of inadequacy, at the bottom, represents intense
discouragement. Students unsuccessful in gaining a sense of significance
or a feeling of belonging at one end of the hierarchy—attention—may
move along that hierarchy to the next and more serious goal of misbehavior, power.

When educators recognize that a student's misbehavior has a purpose
and see the psychological motivation behind his actions,
they can respond in a purposeful and helping manner. They need to
recognize the misbehavior for what it represents—his expression of discouragement, his attempt to gain significance, his effort to belong.

POWER AS A GOAL OF MISBEHAVIOR

Although all four goals of misbehavior are important and should be understood by educators, I would like to single out power struggles in particular. Glasser (1986) identifies the need to gain power as a basic human need. Power, in spite of the cultural taint that it carries is, itself, neither good nor bad (Glasser 1986, pp. 24–25). But efforts to fulfill an unmet need for power can cause conflict between teachers and students. Power struggles represent student misbehavior that not only interferes with classroom learning, but, in fact, often escalates to the point where the building administrator becomes involved.

A student seeking power believes he can be somebody only if he does what he wants to do, and only if he refuses to do what he is supposed to do. Remember this is the youngster's logic here, not the adult's. If a teacher, or even an administrator, tries to teach him a lesson by "pulling him down off his high horse," he only increases the student's underlying sense of inferiority. The student in a power struggle *acts big* to conceal how *small* he really feels. His manifest behavior is just a front to save face.

How do you know when you are having a power struggle with a student? Dinkmeyer and Dinkmeyer, Jr., (1976) state that you need to examine your own feelings toward the student's behavior. In a power struggle, you most often feel angry. You feel provoked. You feel as if your authority has been threatened. You have a tendency to react by either fighting back or by giving in. Let's examine these two common, although ineffective, ways an educator reacts to a power struggle.

Fighting Back

If an educator fights back and is successful in subduing the student, what really has been accomplished? The child defiantly complies, but the relationship between the student and teacher has been hurt. The educator's actions impress upon the child the value of power, and, as such, his desire for more of it is increased. When the child loses to the educator in the power struggle, he learns that it is the powerful who win; therefore if only he had more power, he too could win.

How do students typically deal with losing again and again? Consider, among other actions, rebellion, resentment, striking back (at the teacher or another student who is less powerful), blaming others, apple polishing, bossing others, fear of trying, and lying. In effect, the teacher's efforts to win in the power struggle may backfire (Tjosvold 1976). Schmuck and Schmuck (1979) suggest that students who feel powerless view the classroom as a threatening and insecure place, thus further increasing their feelings of discouragement and further thwarting their efforts to gain significance and to belong.

In reality, though, an adult (teacher or administrator) simply cannot win in a power struggle with a student. Sound strange? Adults must be guided by a sense of responsibility and moral obligation. The student sees no such boundaries, parameters, or rules. The student will use any means to the end of winning in the power struggle. He can be amazingly creative and inventive.

Giving In

What happens if the educator gives in during the power struggle? The student learns, through operant conditioning, that power, in fact, does work. As he has been rewarded by winning, we would expect the student to engage even more frequently in this behavior.

What happens to the child when he wins all the time in these power struggles? He learns to see life as get-get-get; learns his needs are more important than anyone's; feels unloved (after all, how can adults show any real love to a student who constantly wins at their expense); and has difficulties in developing peer relationships.

SUCCESSFUL ALTERNATIVES

It appears that there are only two responses open to a teacher or administrator in a power struggle—fight back or give in. Both of these win-lose reactions have severe, undesirable side effects for both the educator and the child. But is there any other alternative? There are, in fact, several.

Withdraw from the Conflict

One can withdraw from the conflict. Is this just another way of saying giving in? I don't think so. Often when a child finds himself in a power struggle, he would like to get out of the predicament if only he knew how. Unfortunately, he has already committed himself. He has made his challenge, perhaps refusing to do something a teacher has required of him. All of his classmates have seen him make the challenge. He would like to get out of the predicament and at the same time save face.

This is a rather bold statement to make. What makes me believe a student often seeks a face-saving exit from the power struggle? Take your own life, for example. Have you ever been zipping down the interstate, and, for whatever reason, found yourself engaged in a power struggle with another driver? Without really thinking, the other driver cuts you off slightly, so, in turn, you cut him off. The struggle is on.

As you start to think about what you are doing, using all the adult logic you can muster, you ask yourself, "Why am I doing this? We could get killed. Why don't I just stop this silly power struggle?" But it is not so easy to stop the jousting once it has begun.

Think of how you feel when the other driver turns off at the next exit. The power struggle has ended. You feel relieved! His pulling off (withdrawing from the struggle) let the struggle end with both of you saving face.

Further, imagine if you had not "taken up the challenge" in the first place and had just let his cutting in go by unnoticed. Would you be perceived as weak? I think not. In fact, you may even consider yourself quite strong for having resisted the challenge. Thus, withdrawing from a conflict often takes more courage than fighting back. It should not be confused with simply giving in.

Let's take this alternative back to the classroom. Assume we have a student named Billy who has been absent for several days and is frustrated and discouraged at being behind the other students. He misbehaves. He says, with the whole class looking on, "I'm not going to make up all that work; you can't make me!" You feel your authority has been threatened. After all, what will all the other students think if you let Billy get away with this challenge? Note that after Billy has made the challenge he too is thinking about what the rest of the class will think if he knuckles under and does the makeup work. The power struggle is on.

Your first reaction might be, "I'll show you. Just watch me make you do the schoolwork." Or you might think, "It just isn't worth the hassle; I'll give in and let him get out of doing the work." Neither of these are appropriate reactions.

Instead, try withdrawing from the conflict. Don't take up the challenge. Imagine how difficult it will be for the power struggle to go on, let alone escalate, if only one person is involved in the struggle. Suggest a time and place when just you and the student can talk over this problem. Meeting at another, more convenient, time has the added advantage of allowing the problem to be aired in private and not in front of the class as an audience.

When selecting a time and place to meet, be as accommodating as possible to the student's schedule. This may be the first time any adult, especially a teacher, has made such an offer. The student is bound to be a little bit suspicious.

Go into the meeting with the goal of getting your needs met *and* the student's needs met. No one must lose in order for another person to win. Shoot for a win-win outcome. Sit at eye-level with your student; do not tower over him as would be expected of an authority figure. Now is the time to use your very best interpersonal communication problem-solving skills. If you don't have such skills, acquire them!

Those familiar with Thomas Gordon's (1974) *Teacher Effectiveness Training* (T.E.T.) model would probably use Active Listening to help the two of your understand the student's needs and use I-Messages to help convey your needs in a nonblameful manner. At this point, Gordon's skill, Conflict Resolution, would be used. The odds of success—getting your needs and the student's needs met—are high. Remember, this process need only work *once* in order for it to start becoming the norm for how power struggles are handled in the future.

Plan Ahead for Power Struggles

A second response is to plan ahead in anticipation of power struggles. At the start of the year, explain to the students how you plan to handle power struggles when they come up. Explain that it is natural to have such struggles, but that it is important how they are resolved. Point out your logic for the need to save face (on the part of both parties), the need for tempers to calm down, and the need for the power struggles not to interfere with the scheduled learning activities.

Enlist their support for this plan. This effort is typical of the preliminary work that is a must in Glasser's Reality Therapy (1969). If we add to this planning ahead the assumption that students generally perceive school as a good place and that they generally have a good rapport with teachers, withdrawing from a conflict can be a sign of cool-headedness, of strength, of an attempt to see school, like society, as a place where problems must be faced up to and handled in an effective manner.

Another dimension of planning ahead would be to make sure the students understand the bases for your power in the classroom. French and Raven (1960) offer five bases of power for an educator, including legitimate power. This is where students perceive that the teacher has the right to prescribe behavior; the student respects the teacher's social position or office. The students understand that the teacher has a contract to teach and, as such, must by law fulfill these duties. In the heat of a power struggle where personalities are often at odds, it is helpful to refer to the district's expectation that the classes go on as planned and that interruptions be handled at other times. This becomes the reason for "talking about it (a problem) later." It becomes a temporary face-saving out for both the teacher and the student.

Examples of the alternative, plan ahead, are literally endless. Anytime a teacher asks "what if" and then acts accordingly, he or she is planning ahead. What if there are not enough seats for all the children to sit while watching the program in the auditorium? What if more than one child wants to use the paper cutter at the same time? What if a child refuses to makeup his homework? It may be impossible to envision *all* possible situations that can lead to power struggles, but it is not out of the question to consider the more likely situations and then plan accordingly. Successful teachers know that planning ahead pays dividends—whether for a lesson or for a power struggle.

Acknowledge Student Power and Solicit Cooperation

A third response to a power struggle is to help the youngster see how to use his power constructively. This is often done by first acknowledging the actual power the child possesses and then enlisting his voluntary cooperation. This is an extremely powerful response. It works best, as do all attempts at discipline, if students have a rapport with the teacher and generally see school as a good place.

As an example, assume you are an English teacher responsible for the school newspaper. The paper is about to go to press but is missing several critical pictures that still have not been developed by your one and only student photographer. In your attempt to persuade him to get on with this developing task with all due haste, a power struggle emerges. He says, "Well, you know I'm the only one who knows how to develop those pictures, and if I don't do them, there will not be any pictures for the newspaper." You feel angry. You feel provoked. You feel your authority has been threatened. You have all the feelings associated with a power struggle. You are tempted to tell him off, even though you know what he said is absolutely true.

You instead admit the obvious — that he in fact does have the power to determine whether or not the paper will go to press complete with pictures. You then go on to enlist his help or cooperation. You might say, "You are correct, Larry. You are the only one who knows how to develop those pictures. Without your services the newspaper will have to go to print without the pictures. Will you help us by developing the pictures?"

If he agrees, then all you did to get his cooperation was to admit the obvious about his power. Your admitting that he has that power defuses his urge for power, no longer permits him to need to flaunt it, and sets the stage for him not only to become a hero by developing the pictures, but to develop them and save face at the same time.

If you choose to give in to your natural tendency to fight back, you may or may not get the pictures developed. If they are developed with defiant compliance on the student's part, chances are they will be of poor quality. When pictures are needed again, you would not count on Larry. The teacher/student relationship has been damaged. Your admitting the obvious, that Larry possessed power over the immediate situation, was just a sign of significance for him. It was a sign that he has a legitimate place in the group — he belongs.

CONCLUSION

Power struggles are inevitable. What are not inevitable are the ineffective ways educators typically respond to these struggles. Power struggles are also natural. Basic human needs must be fulfilled. The acquisition of power is, "especially for young people, the most difficult (need) to fulfill" (Glasser 1986, p. 27). And yet, for students, "there is no greater work incentive than to be able to see that your effort has a power payoff" (Glasser 1986, p. 27).

Only motivated students engage in power struggles. This is a healthy sign. Channel that need for power. Use the alternatives I have outlined as more effective ways to respond to power struggles.

REFERENCES

Dinkmeyer, D., & Dinkmeyer, D., Jr. (1976). Logical consequences: A key to the reduction of disciplinary problems. *Phi Delta Kappan, 57*(10), 664–666. EJ 139–345.

Dreikurs, R., Grunwald, B., & Pepper, F. (1971). *Maintaining sanity in the classroom: Illustrating teaching techniques.* New York: Harper & Row. Note: the four goals of misbehavior were earlier identified in Dinkmeyer, D., and Dreikurs, R. (1963). *Encouraging children to learn: The encouragement process.* Englewood, NJ: Prentice-Hall.

French, J., Jr., & Raven, B. (1960). The bases for social power. In D. Cartwright, & J. Zander (Eds.), *Group dynamics: Research and theory,* Evanston, IL: Row-Peterson.

Glasser, W. (1969). *Schools without failure.* New York: Harper & Row. See the Chapter III article, "Glasser's Reality Therapy" for more information.

Glasser, W. (1986). *Control theory in the classroom.* New York: Harper & Row.

Gordon, T. (1974). *Teacher effectiveness training.* New York: Peter H. Wyden, Inc.

Schmuck, R., & Schmuck, P. (1979). *Group processes in the classroom.* Dubuque, IA: William C. Brown Company.

Tjosvold, D. (1976, April). *The issue of student control:* A critical review of the literature. Paper presented at the AERA Annual Convention.

Note: The EJ number (306–689) that follows each journal article can be used, in conjunction with the ERIC system described in Chapter IV, to obtain a copy of that article.

NEGATIVE REINFORCEMENT
A Positive Strategy of Classroom Management — Really!

INTRODUCTION

Educators throughout the nation are attempting to respond to the call for better discipline in today's schools. From Gallup Polls of major problems in education published in *Phi Delta Kappan* to the emergence of alternative schools organized around a theme of increased discipline, the message is clear: Educators need better strategies of classroom management. One strategy that teachers and administrators overlook is the positive use of negative reinforcement. This sounds like a contradiction in terms, but it is not!

TWO MAJOR PROBLEMS

Educators face two major problems in taking any corrective action designed to improve classroom discipline. First, they must select a specific theory of classroom management, and second, understand that theory well enough to apply it effectively as a corrective strategy. Teachers can make decisions about the first problem more easily because relatively few theories of classroom management exist. Wolfgang and Glickman (1980, 1986) identify only seven theories running along a continuum from nonintervention strategies to intervention strategies. Specifically, they identify Gordon's TET, Harris's TA, Simon's Values Clarification, Dreikurs's Social Discipline, Glasser's Reality Therapy, Behavior Modification, and Dobson's Punishment.

Of these seven theories that result in classroom management strategies, researchers have written most about behavior modification. As a result, it is behavior modification that educators throughout the nation believe they understand well enough to apply as a corrective strategy. The theory seems as simple as "supply a carrot" for desired behavior and "apply a stick" for undesired behavior. Unfortunately this theory, as well as most other theories of classroom management, is deceptive in its apparent simplicity.

Herein lies the educator's second problem—to understand the theory well enough to apply it regularly as an effective classroom management strategy. The one portion of behavior modification educators least understand, and, as a result, effectively use least is negative reinforcement. They overlook it as a *positive strategy* of classroom management!

NEGATIVE REINFORCEMENT QUIZ

In order to set the stage for a defense of this rather bold assertion about negative reinforcement, readers should take the following quiz before reading further:

NEGATIVE REINFORCEMENT QUIZ

1. If you were doing a crossword puzzle on the subject of "behavior modification" and you were asked for a word that means the same thing as "negative reinforcement," what word would you select?
2. Negative reinforcement usually results in students':
   a. Stopping (decreasing) a behavior the teacher wants stopped.
   b. Starting (increasing) a behavior the teacher wants started.
3. Create an example of negative reinforcement. Try to use an example from your real-life teaching experience.
4. Do you believe students look forward to negative reinforcement?
   a. yes   b. no
5. Do you consciously use positive reinforcement with students?
   a. yes   b. no
6. Do you consciously use negative reinforcement with students?
   a. yes   b. no

GOALS OF BEHAVIOR MODIFICATION

To understand negative reinforcement and appreciate its usefulness as a positive classroom management strategy, one must first understand behavior modification. Behavior modification is reduced to a consideration of the consequences of what a teacher does to modify a student's behavior.

Specifically, what changes in student behavior might a teacher desire? A teacher wants to maintain, to start (increase), or to stop (decrease) student behavior. There are no other choices.

AVAILABLE CONSEQUENCES

Although there is an endless number of specific examples of what a teacher does to modify behavior, all can be grouped into four categories. These categories are defined by whether or not the teacher's response involves supplying or removing a reward, *or* supplying or removing an aversive. These four consequences are known as positive reinforcement (supplying a reward), negative reinforcement (removing an aversive), punishment (supplying an aversive), and time-out (removing a reward/privilege).

TEACHER USE OF CONSEQUENCES

Of the four responses available, most teachers are familiar with and seem to accept positive reinforcement. Punishment, one of the remaining three responses, is often used without a thorough understanding of its side effects. With respect to one of the remaining two responses, time-out, although frequently used this is incorrectly perceived as just another form of punishment. It is the remaining response, negative reinforcement, that is the least understood and least accepted as a strategy, let alone a positive strategy, of classroom management!

How do students respond to these four consequences? Put yourself in the place of the student in the following examples, and imagine the effect upon your behavior that the teacher-supplied consequences would have.

Would you be motivated to start or increase a given behavior if, as a consequence of your behavior, you received a reward? If you had turned in a term paper with an extensive bibliography and earned an "A," would you not be more likely to continue including extensive bibliographies in future term papers? Sure you would! Supplying a reward (something desired by the student) as a consequence of the student's demonstrating a desired behavior is called positive reinforcement. We all use it, it is used on us, and it works.

Suppose, instead, that you were engaged in a behavior where, as a result of that behavior, a reward (more often a privilege) were removed. What effect would that have on you? Most people would either stop, or at least decrease behaviors, where the consequence is to lose a reward. Take the student who clowns in class, and no one, including his peers, pays any attention. Following an expected brief increase in his clowning behavior, the audience notices him less, and his clowning stops. After all, why engage in a behavior that only results in the loss of a reward—attention?

Removing a reward as a consequence of undesired behavior is called time-out.

With the third example, imagine the effect upon the student when, as a result of engaging in a given behavior, the teacher supplies an aversive. Mager (1968) identifies pain, fear and anxiety, frustration, humiliation and embarrassment, boredom, and physical discomfort as typical aversives available to teachers. Supplying an aversive usually has the effect of stopping, or at least reducing, the student's behavior—at least in the presence of the person supplying the aversive.

SCORE: TWO TO ONE

Thus far, we have discussed two responses, time-out and punishment, that have the effect of stopping or reducing a student's behavior. It is presumed that only one response, positive reinforcement, has the effect of starting or increasing a student's behavior. This seems a little lopsided. Teachers would be more successful in modifying student behavior if they had a second response available to start desired student behaviors. And they do! This second response is negative reinforcement. Negative reinforcement accomplishes the same outcome as positive reinforcement—it motivates a student to start or increase a behavior.

The Consequence Grid displayed below summarizes the four categories of responses available to teachers in behavior modification.

CONSEQUENCE GRID

	Teacher SUPPLIES a Consequence	Teacher REMOVES a Consequence
REWARD	POSITIVE REINFORCEMENT	TIME-OUT
(Something valued by student)	Start or increase of student behavior	Stop or decrease of student behavior
AVERSIVE STIMULUS	PUNISHMENT	NEGATIVE REINFORCEMENT
(Something that causes the student mental or physical discomfort)	Stop or decrease of student behavior	Start or increase of student behavior

UNJUSTIFIED CONCERNS

Even if negative reinforcement works, some educators may question whether the end justifies the means. Does not negative reinforcement somehow do some damage? After all, how can something described as "negative" be positive? I suspect we have the same inherent mistrust of "negative reinforcement" as we have of "negative numbers" in mathematics. The mistrust is unjustified. To address these concerns, let us answer the questions asked in the "quiz" displayed earlier.

In question #1, most educators state that "punishment" is a synonym for negative reinforcement. Nothing could be more incorrect. The Consequence Grid clearly shows punishment to be the supplying of an aversive—fear, humiliation, and so on. Negative reinforcement is just the opposite. It is the removal of an aversive.

In question #2, the answer should be "b," starting a behavior the teacher wants started. Note that this is exactly the outcome achieved with positive reinforcement. For question #3, reread your response to see if your example is actually one where the student is encouraged to start or increase a behavior due to the enticement of an aversive's being *removed*.

Question #4 should be answered with a resounding "yes." Who would not look forward to having an aversive removed? Take the child who wishes to get a drink of water (thirst is the aversive), and the teacher says, "Yes, as soon as you can sit quietly for five minutes, you may get a drink." The teacher desires to have the child begin to sit quietly and uses as a consequence the removal of a student-perceived aversive—thirst. This is negative reinforcement. When the child demonstrates the desired behavior (sits quietly for five minutes), the teacher permits the student to get a drink and thus removes the aversive. For questions #5 and #6, far more educators answer "yes" for #5 than for #6. This is unfortunate, as both positive and negative reinforcement accomplish similar results.

TEACHER OPTIONS

Negative reinforcement should be encouraged in the same fashion that one would expect a professional to use the other three consequences available in behavior modification. It does not make much sense to exclude negative reinforcement. Negative reinforcement is just one more option available to educators who choose behavior modification as the basis for classroom management.

EXAMPLES OF NEGATIVE REINFORCEMENT

In order to gain practice with negative reinforcement, the reader should examine the following statements and attempt to identify: (1) the specific behavior the teacher wants modified, and (2), what aversive will be removed if the student demonstrates the desired behavior.

If you are able to complete your work on time for three days in a
row, you will no longer have to stay inside for recess.

If you score eighty percent or higher on the exam, you will not
have to turn in a final paper.

If you get all of your assignments in on time throughout the ten
weeks, you will be able to drop your lowest grade.

If you stay at the assigned task for the entire study period, there
will be no need to phone your parents.

ANALYSIS OF EXAMPLES

In each of the above examples, the student is saddled with an aversive
(or the threat of it). His way out is to change his behavior and do what is
expected of him. If he does, the aversive is lifted, for example, he no
longer has to stay in for recess, his parents will not be called, and so on.
There is no punishment, because no aversive is being supplied. There is no
time-out, because no reward is being removed. And, there is no positive
reinforcement, because no reward is being supplied. What works here is
negative reinforcement — removing an aversive following the demonstration of a desired behavior!

STUDENT TEACHER SURVEY

The negative reinforcement quiz in this article was administered by
Tauber (1988) to over 240 elementary and secondary student teachers,
half from a large land grant university and half from a smaller state-owned
school. The results were disturbingly similar — neither group of soon-to-
be-graduated students understood negative reinforcement.

Seventy percent thought punishment, or a word meaning the same
thing as punishment, was a synonym for negative reinforcement. Sixty-six
percent thought negative reinforcement stopped, not started, behavior.
Ninety-nine percent would regularly consider using positive reinforcement
in the future, yet only thirty-eight percent said the same for negative
reinforcement. When asked why they would use negative reinforcement,
most said something to the effect, "Every once in a while kids need a good
kick in the pants." They had the right answer, but for the wrong reason!

SUMMARY

Without making a value judgment in favor of behavior modification
over any of the other theories of classroom management, I hope that
whatever strategy teachers use, they use it effectively. If behavior modification is their choice, then educators have an obligation to use it properly, and that includes not overlooking the positive effects of negative
reinforcement as a classroom strategy.

Having said this, I believe that when given a choice between supplying positive reinforcement *or* negative reinforcement, both of which accomplish much the same end, you should choose positive reinforcement. A student's living under the pressure of an aversive stimulus *until the teacher chooses to remove it* is fundamentally different from a student's anticipation of a reward.

When given a choice between supplying time-out *or* punishment, both of which also accomplish the same end, you should choose time-out. A student's being supplied an aversive stimulus is fundamentally different from a student's losing a reward. Positive reinforcement and time-out, the preferred teacher-supplied consequences, reduce the potential damage to the all-important ongoing teacher/student relationship.

REFERENCES

Mager, R. (1968). *Developing attitude toward learning.* Palo Alto, CA: Fearon Publishers.

Tauber, R. (1988, February). *Classroom management and negative reinforcement.* Paper presented at the Annual Meeting of the Association of Teacher Educators, San Diego, CA.

Wolfgang, C., & Glickman, C. (1980). *Solving discipline problems.* Boston: Allyn and Bacon, Inc.

Wolfgang, C., & Glickman, C. (1986). *Solving discipline problems.* Boston: Allyn and Bacon, Inc.

Note: Although time-out is defined as the removal of a reward, in practice, time-out is most often supplied by removing a privilege. For instance, my son occasionally forgets to turn off his electric blanket before leaving for school. This is a behavioral pattern I find dangerous and I wish to weaken. His *privilege* of watching television, something he also finds rewarding, is suspended for a specified period of time. The blanket is no longer left on.

SELF-FULFILLING PROPHECY
It Is the Process, Not the Wish, That Makes It So

INTRODUCTION

Teachers' unconscious expectations play a real part in helping to cause the very student discipline problems teachers wish would go away. To the extent that teachers can become conscious of the impact of their expectations on student behaviors, they can prevent many discipline problems from occurring in the first place. Preventing discipline problems is certainly preferable to having to deal with them after they have occurred.

In-service as well as preservice teachers spend endless hours studying operant conditioning (positive reinforcement, negative reinforcement, time-out, punishment, schedules of reinforcement, and so on) with the belief that such an understanding will give them the skills to modify students' behaviors. This is taken for granted. I believe the same argument can be made for teachers' undertaking an exhaustive study of the self-ful-filling prophecy. Although many educators might say they are "familiar" with the self-fulfilling prophecy, few, if any, have studied it with an eye to purposefully using it as a classroom management strategy.

MECHANISM OF THE SELF-FULFILLING PROPHECY

The central idea of the self-fulfilling prophecy (SFP) is that one person's expectation for another's behavior can come to serve as a mecha-nism to help that expectation be fulfilled. How does this happen? Can the SFP as a theory be reduced to such a general statement as "Wishing makes it so"? Is the SFP simply another way of saying the "Power of Posi-tive Thinking"? Does it automatically follow that if you expect a lot (or little) from the students, that is what you will get? The answer to all of these questions is a qualified, "No."

It is true that a wish or expectation is a prerequisite to the operation of the SFP. It is also true that wishes and expectations can be positively correlated with those same expectations coming true. This does not mean, however, that the expectation alone caused the effect of the expectation's being fulfilled.

The SFP is a dynamic *process* that occurs, often unknowingly, between the wish or expectation and its probable fulfillment. As a process, it consists of behaviors, often subtle, but behaviors nevertheless. In order *consciously* to apply the SFP, a teacher must be aware of exactly what the process is and where in the process control can be exerted. How does the process work?

STEPS IN THE SFP PROCESS

1. The teacher forms expectations of particular students regarding their behaviors and achievements.
2. Because of these different expectations, the teacher *behaves* differently toward each student.
3. The teacher's treatment tells each student what behaviors and achievements the teacher expects and thus affects the student's self-concept, achievement motivation, and level of aspiration.
4. If the teacher's treatment is consistent over time, and if the student does not actively resist or change that behavior in some way, it will tend to shape the student's achievement and behavior. High expectation students will tend to achieve at high levels while the achievement of low expectation students will decline.
5. With time, each student's achievements and behaviors will con-form more and more closely to the original prophecy.

As one examines the steps in the process of the self-fulfilling prophecy, one probably has some questions. For instance, "What leads a teacher to form expectations in the first place?" Almost anything could be the source of the expectations—from the student's body build, gender, last name, first name, nickname, facial characteristics, manners (or lack of), personal hygiene, race, hairstyle, anecdotal records, lunchroom rumors, social class, dress, father's occupation, or home address, to the fact that the teacher had the student's "hell-raising" second cousin in class several years ago. Expectations are not, in themselves, damaging *if they are based on fact!*

One might ask, "In what specific ways does a teacher behave differently toward students?" Such differential treatment includes, although certainly is not limited to, proximity, assigning of seats (close to vs. away from the teacher), posture (arms folded vs. a more open stance), touching, facial expressions, assigning classroom responsibilities (for example, changing the calendar, taking attendance to office), tone of voice, setting high or low academic standards, providing opportunities to respond, controlling the amount of time provided to respond, restating or not restating questions in a different form, providing "hints" to the correct answer, and adjusting the frequency, quality, and extent of praise and feedback.

Eden (1986, p. 8) reiterates Rosenthal's four-factor model, which describes how teachers mediate (convey) their expectations to learners. The four factors are CLIMATE, FEEDBACK, INPUT, and OUTPUT. Climate refers to creating a warmer socio-emotional atmosphere. Often this is accomplished nonverbally. Feedback refers to the extent of specific information provided as to how well the learner has completed a task. Input refers to how much teaching of new material takes place. Output refers to giving the learner more opportunities to respond and to seek clarification.

Take, for example, Joe, a student of mine of whom I have relatively *low* expectations. He comes to my office and asks, "Are you busy?" I say, "Yes, but come on in" (Climate). He asks how he did on the first draft of his term paper, and I say, "OK, about average." He leafs through the paper only to find very few marginalia comments (Feedback). I neglect to inform him of several good resources in the library he could obtain (I don't think he would take the time and effort to get them, anyhow) (Input). An uncomfortable pause follows whereby Joe gets the message that he is not going to find out a whole lot more, so what is the use of asking (Output). He leaves. Have my expectations and corresponding actions actually contributed to Joe's meeting my low expectations of him? I think so.

On the other hand, look at what happened with Larry, someone of whom I have very high expectations. He comes to my office and asks, "Are you busy?" I say "I always have time for talking with you, Larry" (Climate). He asks how he did on the first draft of his term paper. I go on to identify several specific points that made the paper strong and also point out several areas that he should work on to improve the paper (Feedback). I then proceed to instruct him in the proper way to interpret a correlation coefficient, an error he made in his paper (Input). Finally, I ask, "Do you have any questions concerning what you need to work on to improve the paper?" He responds by asking for clarification on two points (Output). He leaves. Is there any doubt that Larry senses the high expectations I have for him? Is there any doubt that my actions will help Larry meet these expectations? There is no doubt.

Before reading further, take a moment and reflect upon situations in your own life where you may have acted toward students as I did toward Joe and Larry. Consider your motivations for doing so. Is it possible that your actions contributed to your students' living *up to* or *down to* your expectations of them? While reflecting, think of those times in your life where people have had high and low expectations of you. Did their expectations, and their behavior toward you that followed, affect you? This is what it is all about.

The vast majority of these differential behaviors occur unconsciously, without any intended malice toward the students. Study after study have shown that teachers simply are not aware of the subtle differences in behavior they display toward high expectation vs. low expectation students. Certainly, if a teacher's plan is to use the SFP as a classroom management tool, he must first be aware of how easy it is to engage in such differential behaviors without even knowing it.

Another question often asked is, "How long would it take before the expectations might be fulfilled?" A number of variables could affect the answer, including: how strong a self-concept and sense of identity the student already possesses prior to the teacher's expectations (and subsequent differential behaviors), to what degree the expectations of the teacher are congruent with those of the student's significant others (for example, parents, peers), and to what degree the student has the opportunity to come in contact with other educators whose prophecies may differ.

Finally, one might ask, "To what extent do the teacher's prophecies actually come true, or is it just that teachers see what they expect to see and then evaluate accordingly?" Empirical studies have shown that when students are randomly assigned, without the teacher knowing it, to higher expectation and lower expectation groups, the end result is that the higher expectation students, in fact, tend to perform at higher levels, and lower expectation students, in fact, tend to perform at lower levels. The increase or decrease in the students' level of performance is *not* just a figment of the teacher's imagination—it actually happens, and all evidence confirms that the teacher's own expectations and subsequent differential behaviors helped make it happen!

To make matters worse, evidence shows that when lower expectation students do achieve beyond what was expected of them, teachers often rank them on personal characteristics as being less likeable and less socially conforming. They are penalized for doing better than expected. When lower expectation students do achieve, either teachers have to admit that their expectations were wrong, *or* argue that the lower expectation students' surprising achievements were just a fluke, due to cheating, and so on. Admitting that one's expectations might not be correct does not come easily to teachers, for they, like the rest of the human community, do not like to be proven wrong.

A teacher's differential treatment, though often subtle, apparently is obvious enough to be picked up *and modeled* by higher expectation students (usually also higher achieving students, though it is not clear which came first the achievement or the expectations). These higher expectation students soon start to mirror the teacher's differential behaviors toward the lower expectation students. Now the lower expectation students have it coming to them from all angles—the die is cast.

SELECTED SFP STUDIES

In order to impress upon the reader how false beliefs (expectations with little or no foundation in fact) can result in unfair and invalid stereotypes, I will highlight several SFP studies—each of which relates to our nation's preoccupation with body build.

Lerner (1969), in a study on body build–behavior relationships, concluded that, all other things being equal, a male's body build (thin, normal, heavy) influences the expectations of others. The following results were significant at the $p < .001$ level. Respondents "expected" that thin people were most likely to have nervous breakdowns, to make poor fathers, to make the poorest doctors, and to endure pain the least. In contrast, heavy persons are "expected" to be the poorest athletes, need friends the most, and be least likely to be chosen leader. A mesomorph (normal build) is "expected" to be most preferred as a friend, make the best soldier, to put his own interests before others, and to be elected leader. It is easy to hypothesize who, simply due to body build, has the edge in school, in the job market, in politics (consider, for example, recent presidential candidates), and so on.

A 1972 study by Staffier, entitled "Body Build and Behavioral Expectancies in Young Females" reported remarkably similar findings for females as were found by Lerner (1969) for males. Staffier reported that those with a mesomorph or normal body build are seen as all things favorable. All significant ($p < .01$) adjectives assigned to the normal build silhouettes were favorable—best friend, kind, lots of friends, remembers, healthy, brave, smart and neat.

Children are not the only victims of the SFP. Bonuso (1983), in an article entitled "Body Type: A Factor in the Hiring of School Leaders," studied the effects of height and weight on would-be administrators' chances of being hired as high school principals. Superintendents (N = 475) rated both males and females who were tall and of ideal weight significantly higher than individuals of the same sex but of other stature types ($p < .05$).

The point to these examples is to highlight whether body build, alone, or if at all, is a valid indicator of future behavior? Of course not. Heavy males *can* be good parents. Heavy females *can* be smart, brave, and neat. Short, thin, female administrators *can* be effective high school principals. But, what chance do they have *if* the public already has formed its expectations of them based upon their body build, and then they go on to act accordingly.

Before everyone runs off to the local gym or buys Jane Fonda's latest workout video in order to get back in shape, keep in mind that body build is only one of many, *many* human characteristics from which expectations are formed (and misformed). Similar research on expectations could be cited for children coming from single as opposed to two-parent families, or children who look more, rather than, less Mexican or black as it relates to predicted achievement. It could be cited for males as against females with respect to anticipated competence in mathematics or choice of careers. It could be cited for minority children vs. middle-class white children with respect to predicted grade point average. It could be cited for vocational and academic students with respect to being judged "college material." And, as unfair as it may be, there is evidence that expectations are also based upon children's attractiveness and first names. Unfortunately, the examples are endless!

SFP: A TWO-WAY STREET

The SFP can consciously and regularly be applied by a teacher to students, *and* it can be just as easily applied by students to teachers. As a teacher, have you ever had a class in which you could immediately sense that the students expected the course to be a good one, and, as a result, you put in that extra effort, time, and creativity to make the course live up to the students' expectations. Before anyone knew it, the class, in fact, turned out to be just as good, if not better, than the students had originally prophesied. It is clear that neither teachers nor students play Pygmalion exclusively in the classroom. If only students realized the power they possess through positive (or negative) expectations to influence the quality of any given class or course.

CONCLUSION

At this point some teachers may be reluctant to form any expectations at all for fear of misusing the self-fulfilling prophecy. Unfortunately, it is impossible to avoid forming expectations. Our only defense against the SFP is to be as sure as possible that our expectations are based on solid evidence, *and* continually to realize that we play a definite role in the process of fulfilling our expectations. Teachers need to understand the SFP well enough not only to keep it in check, but consciously to use it as one more classroom management tool.

REFERENCES

Bonuso, C. (1983). Body type: A factor in the hiring of school leaders. *Phi Delta Kappan, 64*(5), 374. No EJ number cited.

Eden, D. (1986). OD and the self-fulfilling prophecy: Boosting productivity by raising expectations. *The Journal of Applied Behavioral Science, 22*(1), 1–13. No EJ number cited.

Lerner, R. (1969). The development of stereotyped expectancies of body build–behavior relations. *Child Development, 40*(1), 137–141. EJ 003-248.

Staffier, J. (1972). Body build and behavioral expectancies in young females. *Developmental Psychology, 6*(1), 125–127. No EJ number cited.

Note: The EJ number (for example, EJ 306-689) that follows each journal article can be used, in conjunction with the ERIC system described in Chapter IV, to obtain a copy of that article.

MASLOW'S HIERARCHY
Your Role in Students' Meeting Their Deficiency Needs and *Vice Versa*

INTRODUCTION

Everyone seems to have heard of Maslow's Hierarchy of Needs with its characteristic pyramid shape, ranging from physiological needs at the bottom through self-actualization needs at the top. This section will not be a rehash of that model but, instead, will concentrate upon how the model has specific applications to establishing and/or maintaining classroom discipline.

Maslow's hierarchy can be a powerful teacher tool to help avoid discipline problems occurring in the first place. Unfortunately it is too often simply a bit of psychological theory that everyone has heard of *but* few consciously use as a classroom management strategy.

So that everyone has the same information base, a Maslow-type pyramid follows on next page and a brief explanation of the model is provided. Following this explanation, the specifics of how the model can be used as a common-sense classroom management strategy will be addressed.

SOME GIVENS

1. Maslow's Hierarchy represents a model based upon the observation of healthy people—just like you and me. Too often theoretical models in psychology are designed to describe deviants from "normal" behavior and, thus, are of less practical use to practitioners such as teachers. Teachers need theories that work for most children, most of the time, in most situations.

2. Unlike other researchers such as Murray (1938), who identified over forty separate needs, Maslow limited his categories of needs to a manageable number.

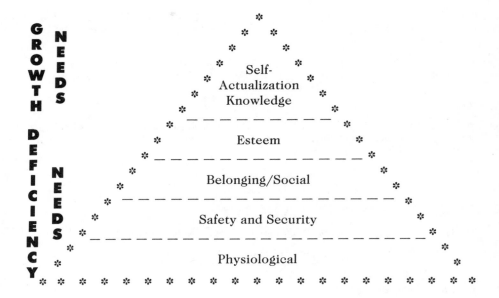

3. Maslow maintains that lower needs are prepotent to higher needs. This means that human beings will be less motivated by higher needs *until* lower needs are either met or perceived to be well on their way to being met. It is no surprise, for instance, that reduced or free lunch programs are pedagogically sound ideas, so that the study of Shakespeare and quadratic equations will not be supplanted by hunger pangs and growls.

4. Maslow states that only unmet needs motivate. The implications of this statement are far-reaching as one considers using Maslow's Hierarchy as a strategy for classroom management.

5. Finally, Maslow (1968) groups his hierarchical needs into two categories—Deficiency Needs and Growth Needs. Deficiency Needs encompass physiological, safety, belonging/social, and esteem. Growth Needs encompass knowledge and self-actualization. It is this dichotomy that serves as the primary basis for my argument concerning the use of Maslow's Hierarchy as a classroom management tool.

DEFICIENCY NEEDS VS. GROWTH NEEDS

In order to understand how teachers can use Maslow's Hierarchy as a classroom management tool, teachers must note several key differences between Growth Needs and Deficiency Needs. Four of these differences are summarized as follows:

1. Deficiency Needs are basic needs—common to all human beings. Growth Needs are more idiosyncratic—unique to each individual.

2. Deficiency Need gratification tends to be episodic (for example, eating three meals a day, sleeping every night, needing repeated evidence that you are succeeding at a task). Growth Needs are continuous and never ending (for example, the feeling that you have when reading a good book—please don't let it ever end).
3. Deficiency needs can only be satisfied by other people (for example, one relies on a police force for protection, one gets into a club only by the invitation of others, the evaluation of one's work is dependent upon what others think of it). Growth Needs are satisfied more autonomously and independently.
4. A Deficiency Need–motivated person tends to be more dependent upon others, whom he sees primarily as need gratifiers (for example, "If I could only date the football captain, that would make me popular"; or "If I hang around with that group, will others think I am a nerd?") Growth Need–motivated persons see others as individuals in their own right.

It would make a teacher's job much easier if *all* students were motivated by Growth Needs. Students would have an insatiable appetite for knowledge and would be constantly trying to become the best person they are capable of becoming. Teachers would be in teacher-heaven. Unfortunately, Deficiency Needs are prepotent to Growth Needs. This means that students spend much of their time and energy, in and out of school, day in and day out, trying to meet Deficiency Needs. How can teachers capitalize upon this state of affairs?

When teachers realize that students' Deficiency Needs can only be met by others, *and then* realize that they (teachers) often are those "others," they have the basis for a powerful classroom management tool. Teachers, by virtue of their leadership and evaluative roles, are in a prime position to assist students in meeting their Deficiency Needs. *As long as students believe they are meeting their Deficiency Needs through socially acceptable means, they have little reason to misbehave.* Misbehavior, itself, is often a student's misguided effort to get unmet needs met. For instance, is there any doubt that the class clown, who successfully disrupts your teaching, is actually getting his/her needs met? When provided with socially acceptable ways of meeting their needs, students will choose good behavior over misbehavior.

Teachers can do many things that can help students meet their Deficiency Needs. For instance, physiological needs can be met by the school, if not by a single teacher, by providing nutritious and appealing lunches, some at relatively low cost. Teachers can control the temperature and flow of air in a classroom. Snack times, access to water fountains, and lavatory privileges are under the teacher's control.

Safety and security needs can be met by providing a detailed syllabus, making specific assignments, and explaining exactly how one will be evaluated. Crossing guards, playground supervisors, and hall monitors can be provided. Having class favorites and losing one's temper (205-pound adult goes temporarily berserk in class) can be avoided.

Teachers can help students meet their belonging/social needs in many ways; after all, the school is a miniature community in and of itself. Individual classrooms can work hard as a team to earn the school award for least absences, for the most mothers and fathers attending parents' night, for most Campbell's soup labels collected (traded in toward computer equipment). Taking turns assigning responsibility for changing the calendar, passing out the snack, and taking notes to the office show that all students have an important place in the group. Bulletin boards with all students in the class identified on leaves for the fall season show all who belong. Displaying pictures of the class engaged in common activities throughout the year stresses the social nature of the classroom. Pep rallies can help bolster team spirit; trophy cases prominently displayed in the school's entrance can do likewise.

Esteem needs can be met by providing students the opportunity to display their uniqueness and individuality. Show-and-tell time might provide this opportunity. Having students share with the class their special hobbies lets them feel special. Keeping informed as to what one's students have done, both in and out of school (for example, earned a merit badge, having been accepted by a college, being selected paper carrier for the month), and then sharing that information with the entire class once again allows individual students to be singled out.

It bears repeating: If students are provided with socially acceptable avenues of meeting their deficiency needs, they will choose to do so rather than misbehave. Teachers are in a prime position to help students do just that.

The fact that Deficiency Needs are episodic only means that these needs cannot be met once and for all. One cannot get enough food today to last a lifetime. One cannot use the benefit of a crossing guard one day and have that one instance last forever. One cannot be accepted into a single group and feel a sense of belonging for all time. Deficiency Needs must be repeatedly met, day after day. Luckily for students, teachers are with students day after day. As teachers, let's use this to our benefit, and to our students' benefit, by helping them meet their Deficiency Needs. The end result will be fewer discipline problems *and* greater learning.

WHAT'S SAUCE FOR THE GOOSE . . .

If it has not dawned on the reader yet, students are not the only ones expending time and energy on a daily basis trying repeatedly to meet their Deficiency Needs. Teachers, too, like the rest of the world, are motivated by Deficiency Needs. Just as teachers make up a significant part of the "others" in a student's world, students make up a significant part of the "others" in a teacher's world. Teachers depend upon students to help them (teachers) meet their Deficiency Needs.

Without students, teachers would have no job (security need) and thus no income to buy food and provide shelter (physiological need).

Without students, there would be no career for teachers to be part of (belonging/social). Without feedback from students, teachers would never know for sure, one way or the other, whether they possess unique qualities (esteem).

Teachers need students just as much as students need teachers. To most readers, the "fact" of this statement is no revelation. A more correct statement, conveying the reason behind the "fact," would be teachers need students to meet their Deficiency Needs just as much as students need teachers to meet their Deficiency Needs. Let's use Maslow's Hierarchy and our knowledge of Deficiency Needs as a strategy of classroom management. Help students meet their legitimate needs, and you will have significantly fewer discipline problems to deal with.

P.S. I call your attention to the article in this chapter by Dreikurs where four goals of misbehavior (attention, power, revenge, inadequacy) are identified. Please note that each of these goals is dependent upon the student's faulty belief that he can only BELONG (one of Maslow's basic needs) if he seeks one of these goals. If the student felt he BELONGED, he would have no need to misbehave. Help him belong. Help him meet his Deficiency Needs.

REFERENCES

Maslow, A. (1968). *Toward a psychology of being.* New York: Van Nostrand Reinhold Company.

Maslow, A. (1970). *Motivation and personality* (2d ed.). New York: Harper & Row.

Murray, H. (1938). *Explorations in personality; A clinical and experimental study of fifty men of college age.* New York: Oxford University Press.

CLASSICAL CONDITIONING
The Goodrich of Conditioning

INTRODUCTION

"Close your books, take out a sheet of paper, and number 1–20. We (you) are going to take a TEST." Palms turn sweaty, faces become flushed, stomach muscles tighten, guilt feelings surface — all at the sound of that four-letter word, "test." Worse yet, these feelings and associated physiological changes occur without our ability to resist.

Classical conditioning is the Goodrich equivalent of the tire industry. Everyone has heard of Goodyear — they have the blimp. But how many have heard of Goodrich? So, too, it is with classical conditioning and operant conditioning — the latter being the well known one of the pair.

Far more textbook space is devoted to, and many more journal articles are written about, operant conditioning than classical conditioning. Numerous college courses and in-service programs center around the principles of operant conditioning and its associated vocabulary — behavior modification, shaping, contingency management, token economies, positive reinforcement, negative reinforcement, time-out, punishment, successive approximations, schedules of reinforcement, and so on. This is definitely not so for classical conditioning.

Yet operant conditioning is responsible for learning in only one area — the cognitive domain. Bloom's (1956) Cognitive Taxonomy: knowledge, understanding, application, analysis, synthesis, and, at times, evaluation, typifies this domain. The two other areas of learning are the affective domain and the psychomotor domain. These three domains can be summarized as cognitive (knowing), affective (feeling), and psychomotor (doing). Classical conditioning is the primary method of learning in the affective domain. As such, educators have a responsibility to understand classical conditioning and to be able to apply it with the same degree of expertise as they do operant conditioning.

The three domains are often separated for purposes of study, but in real life they overlap. Is a student's difficulty in geometry due to a lack of understanding (cognitive), feelings of anxiety (affective), or an inability to properly manipulate a protractor or compass (psychomotor)? More than likely, it is a combination of the three.

Although the author recognizes the importance of all three domains, the remainder of this paper will focus upon the affective domain. However, one cannot do justice to the affective domain without a clear understanding of classical conditioning.

CLASSICAL CONDITIONING: SOME BACKGROUND

Classical conditioning consists of a set of actions by which one stimulus comes to substitute for another in *evoking* or *eliciting* a response — often physiological in nature. In a classroom, the "set of actions" are under the control of the teacher, among others. The words "evoke" and "elicit" reinforce the involuntary (no way to resist) nature of classical conditioning.

Most readers know of the Pavlovian experiment. At first, when an experimenter rings a bell as a stimulus, nothing happens (no reaction) on the part of the hungry subject animal. But after repeated pairings of the ringing bell with the presentation of food powder (guaranteed to cause saliva to flow), the experimenter need only present the ringing bell and the animal salivates. The animal has been classically conditioned to respond to the sound of the bell — a previously neutral stimulus. The animal hears the bell, anticipates the food powder, and the saliva flows. It is almost that simple.

What does this have to do with children in school? Lots! For example, through classical conditioning, the word "test," a previously neutral stimulus, can acquire the ability to elicit fear and anxiety. The words, "Next week you will give your speech without notecards"; the very sight of a physical education teacher who requires everyone to "climb the rope"; and simply walking by the principal's office—all can produce similar feelings. Situation after situation exists where a previously neutral stimulus comes to substitute for another stimulus in causing a response.

Not all examples of classical conditioning result in bad feelings, such as fear and anxiety. Surely there are some students who have good feelings when they hear the word "test," look forward with confidence to giving their speech "without notecards," and think the principal is a real neat person. Classical conditioning is responsible for students learning both these good and bad feelings. As teachers, we must understand classical conditioning well enough to use it as a tool to increase the former and decrease the latter.

A FAMILIAR EXAMPLE OF CLASSICAL CONDITIONING

I regularly place students in local schools for semester-long sophomore field experiences, wherein each cooperating teacher is visited several times throughout the semester. I usually stop at a teacher's door, knock lightly, and wait until the teacher comes out in the hall to talk with me. It is not uncommon, nor unexpected, for the teacher's students to become restless and to begin to talk. Sure enough, the teacher will reach inside the classroom, and . . . well, you know what the teacher does, don't you? She flicks the light switch. Apparently, flicking the lights on and off is a shorthand message that means, "Stop talking while I am talking with Dr. Tauber, or there is going to be h--- to pay when I come back into the room."

How did students learn what flicking the lights on and off meant? They learned it primarily through classical conditioning. What specific set of events caused the learning to take place? One day, early in the school year, the teacher got fed up with the noise level and flicked the lights on and off as she yelled, "Quiet!" After this pairing took place several times, students perceived the connection between "Quiet!" and the lights being turned on and off. Soon, the teacher needed only to turn off the lights (previously a neutral stimulus), and the students anticipated the screaming of "Quiet!" Anticipating the word "Quiet!" evoked or elicited their settling-down behavior.

Be aware that, as familiar as the above example is, it does not guarantee that teachers understand the foundational principle of classical conditioning that makes it all work. And, if teachers do not understand the basic principle, then they are ill prepared to apply the principle in other situations consciously and regularly.

REINFORCEMENT: WHAT PLACE IN CLASSICAL CONDITIONING?

What does a teacher do in classical conditioning to reinforce certain student feelings (for example, feeling good about mathematics, finding pleasure in reading)? One's first response might be, "I thought the term reinforcement only applied to operant conditioning—for example, gold stars, M&Ms, high grades." In fact, reinforcement applies to classical conditioning just as much as it does to operant conditioning.

In classical conditioning, reinforcement refers to the periodic pairing of the two stimuli that were paired in the first place. In my flick-the-light-switch example, reinforcement would consist of the teacher's periodically screaming "Quiet!" when she flicked the lights. Renewing the connection between the two stimuli is what is meant by reinforcement.

EXTINCTION: A SYNONYM FOR AVOIDANCE?

What does a teacher do in classical conditioning in order to help extinguish certain student feelings (for example, fear of mathematics, displeasure in reading, reluctance to give a speech)? Too often the student simply tries to avoid the stimulus that is causing the fear, displeasure, or reluctance. Avoidance *does not* lead to extinction.

A family member of mine, for example, was scared at the age of sixteen by a snake dangling from a tree branch over her head while she swung on a swing. To this day, she is still petrified of snakes, even though she has avoided them in real life and in pictures for over half a century. The fear is still there.

How, then, does one extinguish unwanted feelings? There are three recognized steps to do this. Collectively, the steps are known as "desensitizing."

1. Get the person involved in the anxiety-producing behavior in small, manageable increments.
2. Surround the person with pleasurable competing stimuli.
3. Anticipate where negative feelings might be "learned" through classical conditioning and act preventively.

Almost any anxiety-producing task can be broken down into smaller, more manageable tasks. Students fearful of giving a speech before a group can be asked to deliver the speech before a mirror, then to one other student, then to a small group of peers, and then before a larger group.

Examine your school environment to determine where students show such fear and anxiety. How could you break the larger task down into more manageable components? I do this myself as I watch horror movies on television. They scare me to death. Rather than avoid horror movies altogether, I keep the remote control in my hands and quickly change the station at the real scary parts (shower curtain about to be pulled back where the villain has the knife raised). A moment later, I switch back to the program. Slowly, I have been able to overcome much of my fear, and now I can sit through the scariest movie using the remote control only once or twice.

People are often taught exercises that help them to relax when they encounter anxiety-producing situations. Teachers can go out of their way to create a comfortable, inviting area where students can practice their reading. Mathematics and science can be taught in a way (for example, *Mr. Wizard*) that is more pleasurable. The Olympics can be used as a sort of backdrop for physical education instructors who are asking students to try the vault, climb the rope, or tread water. The campus where I teach is well groomed and beautifully situated. Even on those days when I have something scheduled that I might dread doing, just walking across campus, saying "hello" to friends, and recognizing familiar landmarks, help to reduce the anxiety.

Finally, as with most any circumstance, "An ounce of prevention is worth a pound of cure." Taking the time and effort to anticipate where negative feelings might be "learned" and acting preventively are a must. Does it come as a surprise that students might well be fearful of giving speeches; doing a term paper; moving to the junior high; carrying messages to the principal's office; scheduling statistics, trigonometry, or calculus; and studying Shakespeare? Of course not. Knowing what we now know about classical conditioning, teachers should act to head off negative feelings before they are formed in the first place.

THERE IS PAIRING, AND THEN THERE IS PAIRING

Pairing two stimuli, one previously neutral and one previously capable of eliciting a response, is the essence of classical conditioning. But exactly how should teachers go about pairing these two stimuli in order to maximize their effect? Several choices exist.

Assume we call any previously neutral stimulus the Conditioned Stimulus (CS). This is the stimulus we wish to condition the learner to respond to. Flicking the lights on and off would be an example of a CS. Further, assume we call any stimulus already capable of evoking our desired response an Unconditioned Stimulus (UCS). This stimulus already possesses the ability to elicit the response we want. Screaming "Quiet!" would be an example of a UCS.

What different ways could we pair a UCS and a CS? We could present the two simultaneously; we could present the UCS before the CS; and we could present the CS before the UCS. All of a sudden things get a little complicated. I apologize for that, but if teachers are going to use classical conditioning in a purposeful fashion, they have a responsibility to use it correctly.

If we present the UCS and the CS at the same time, the learner will pay no attention to the CS. Why should he? After all, when a teacher screams "Quiet," simultaneously there are a million other CS (neutral stimuli) lurking about—ceiling lights, painted walls, calendar on the wall, gerbils in a cage, floor tiles, teacher's clothes, and so on.

If we present the UCS before the CS, the learner will note the UCS ("Quiet!"), and it will instantly trigger or evoke a response. Once again, the CS (flicking the lights) will either not be noticed at all or, if noticed, will be seen as having little relationship to the UCS.

The correct way to pair the two stimuli is to present the CS just a moment before the UCS. Flicking the lights on and off and then quickly saying "Quiet!" would be the most effective way to pair the two. Flicking the lights is noticed because it comes first. It is remembered long enough so that the student begins to associate the flicking of the lights with the screaming of the word "Quiet!" which follows. After repeated pairings, flicking the lights causes the student to anticipate the word "Quiet!" which in turn evokes the desired response of settling down.

SUMMARY

Classical conditioning is responsible for students' positive-type feelings and negative-type feelings whether directed towards subject matter, peers, teachers, or education in general. The principles of classical conditioning work whether or not *we* make them work. Why not use classical conditioning as a tool for your benefit and for the students' benefit? Ringness (1976) asked the question more than a decade ago, "Whatever happened to the study of classical conditioning?" Apparently, not much has happened. Let's remedy that situation.

REFERENCE

Bloom, B. (Ed.) (1956). *Taxonomy of educational objectives, Handbook I: Cognitive Domain,* NY: McKay.
Ringness, T. (1976). Whatever happened to the study of classical conditioning? *Phi Delta Kappan, 57*(7), 447; 455. EJ 132-525.

Note: The EJ number above (EJ 132-525) can be used, in conjunction with the ERIC system described in Chapter IV, to obtain a copy of the article.

GORDON'S TEACHER (PARENT) EFFECTIVENESS TRAINING
Active Listening and I-Messages

INTRODUCTION

Two interpersonal communication problems regularly occur in the classroom—how to respond when a student owns a problem, and how to respond when the teacher owns a problem. In the first case, the student's behavior is acceptable to the teacher; it does not interfere with the teacher's meeting his needs. Here, the teacher's goal is to help that student. In the second case, the student's behavior is not acceptable to the teacher; it interferes with the teacher's meeting his needs. The teacher wants to help himself. Different, yet precise, responding skills are required in each case. More effective teachers have a model to which they refer in order to help them decide what skill to use when. Gordon's *Teacher Effectiveness Training* (T.E.T.) is such a model.

T.E.T.: SOME BACKGROUND

The "E.T." in T.E.T. does not stand for that lovable extraterrestrial being that was the big smash at the cinema several years ago; it stands for "Effectiveness Training." Effectiveness Training is used, not in the generic sense whereby the reader may assign his own meaning to it, but in a specific sense referring to a communication model designed by Thomas Gordon. His model is an example of a humanistic ideology being translated into a complete, as well as consistent, set of practical skills.

The model was first described in Gordon's book, *Parent Effectiveness Training* (1970). This was followed by *Teacher Effectiveness Training* (1974), and, most recently, by *Leader Effectiveness Training* (1977). The general applicability of the model exists due to the similarities in all interpersonal relationships and the corresponding need for communication skills, whether the relationship is parent/child, teacher/student, or manager/employee.

The Effectiveness Training model describes the *process* of communication between two people. This process transcends geography as well as time.

T.E.T.: THE MODEL

The Effectiveness Training model is best represented by a rectangle or window through which one views the behaviors of all other people. The top part of the window depicts behaviors of the other person (for example, student, fellow teacher, head teacher) that you find "acceptable." The bottom part of the rectangle depicts behaviors of the other person that you find "unacceptable." This is the first decision the user of the model must make: Are the other person's behaviors "acceptable" or "unacceptable"?

According to Gordon, "acceptable" means that the other person's behavior does not interfere with your meeting your needs. It does not mean that you give your blessing to the behavior or that, necessarily, you wish it would continue. "Unacceptable" means that the other person's behavior does interfere with your meeting your needs. It does not mean that you find the behavior to be repugnant or immoral; you would just like it stopped.

We normally have little difficulty identifying examples of both categories of behaviors. The dividing line separating the "acceptable" category

T.E.T.: THE MODEL

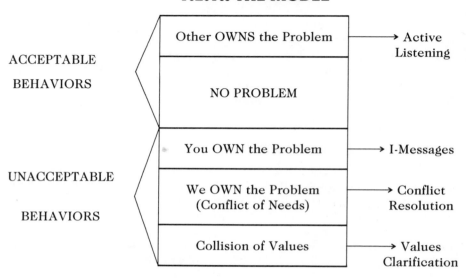

from the "unacceptable" category is fluid; it moves up and down. Self, others, and environment all affect the line's movement. There are days when you (self) feel especially good, all is going well. Lots of behaviors of the other person are judged to be "acceptable." On those days when, for whatever reason, you don't feel so good, the line moves up; far fewer behaviors are judged to be "acceptable," many more are "unacceptable."

Others, themselves, influence the line. Teachers are simply more or less accepting of some students than of others. It is not being unprofessional; it is simply being human. It could be how these others dress, act, respond in class, or attend to personal hygiene that causes teachers to be more or less accepting of their behaviors. Reasons aside, the fact is, it happens. We cannot be equally accepting all the time of all of our students (bosses, friends, peers). It would be an extra-human task to do so.

Finally, the environment in which the other's behavior occurs influences whether or not it will be acceptable. An "acceptable" student behavior that occurs when the principal is not observing may, all of a sudden, be judged "unacceptable" when the principal walks into the classroom.

It is crucial to use the window/rectangle to decide first whether the other person's behavior is "acceptable" or "unacceptable." Gordon identifies one responding skill for the former and another responding skill (actually, several) for the latter. The best of responding skills, proficiently applied, are of little value if the circumstances surrounding the situation do not warrant that particular response. The responding skill must be congruent with the initial "acceptable"/"unacceptable" decision.

In the top part of the window, the "acceptable" behavior area, there are times when a responding skill is warranted AND times when one is not warranted. When the other person's behavior is deemed "acceptable" and the other person shows no sign of experiencing a problem, then no responding skill is necessary. It is in this part of the model that maximum student learning can take place. This is the "no problem" area. The goal of the T.E.T. model is to enlarge this "no problem" area.

On the other hand, when the other person's behavior is deemed "acceptable," but it is obvious that that person is experiencing a problem, then a responding skill is necessary. Although people may not come right out and say they are experiencing a problem, they often give verbal and/or nonverbal signals that such is the case. People experiencing a problem act atypically. They may cry, sulk, scream; give curt responses; express feelings of sadness, bitterness, disappointment, frustration; and more. All of these are cues that the person is experiencing a problem IF these represent unusual behaviors for this person. Here we have a situation where you can "accept" the other person's behavior (he does have the right to cry, to be disappointed, and so on, doesn't he?), but you want to facilitate his solving his problem. Remember, he owns the problem; it belongs to him.

PRACTICE WITH "OTHER OWNS THE PROBLEM" SITUATIONS

In the following situations, assume that you accept the other person's behavior, what they are saying or doing does not tangibly interfere with your meeting your needs. At the same time, though, it is obvious the other person is experiencing a problem. You want to help. What would you say in response to Mr. Gamble's and Eileen's problems? Some suggested responses appear later in the article.

#1 You are eating lunch in the faculty room. Mr. Gamble, a fellow teacher, comes up to you and says, "Nothing I do with my students seems to work. I'm not sure I'm cut out to be a teacher. What do you think?"

#2 You have a primary student named Eileen who usually works extra hard to overcome her lack of natural ability in mathematics. When you ask her why she is not working on her math assignment, she responds by saying, "This work is too hard. I can't do it. I am just too stupid!"

If you are anything like the rest of the human community, in spite of good intentions, you probably responded with what Gordon calls "Roadblocks to Communication." Their net effect is to close off the very communication you wanted to enhance; the very communication that could help the other person come to grips with, and possibly solve, his problem. Roadblocks not only cause the other person to want to escape your presence, they also make it less likely he will seek you out as a listener the next time he has a problem.

ROADBLOCKS TO COMMUNICATION

There are twelve Roadblocks to Communication. They are: (1) Ordering, Directing; (2) Admonishing, Threatening; (3) Moralizing, Preaching; (4) Advising, Giving Solutions; (5) Lecturing, Giving Logical Arguments; (6) Judging, Criticizing; (7) Praising, Agreeing; (8) Ridiculing, Shaming; (9) Analyzing, Diagnosing; (10) Sympathizing, Consoling; (11) Probing, Questioning, Interrogating; and (12) Withdrawing, Humoring.

Several response categories sound as if they would be obvious Roadblocks to Communication (for example, Threatening, Criticizing, Ridiculing), while other response categories (for example, Praising, Giving Solutions, Consoling) seem, at least at first glance, to be quite appropriate ways of responding. Let's examine further some of these seemingly appropriate response categories.

Take, for example, Giving Solutions. When another person owns a problem, giving solutions should be avoided. How committed to your solution for his problem do you expect the other person will be? Not very. If your solution does not work, who takes the blame? You do. After all, it was your solution. If the solution actually does work, how does the person who had the problem feel? Initially, relieved, but later, perhaps a little humiliated. Why the possibility of humiliation? With some additional thought it becomes obvious that if he had been given the chance to talk out the problem, he, too, may have come up with a solution—maybe even a better solution than yours. Do we so readily offer solutions because it makes us, as the solution giver, feel good? Do we feel that, unless we offer solutions, we haven't been of any help? Do we offer solutions because we do not have enough faith in the other person's ability to come up with his own? If we keep handing people solutions, when, if ever, will they develop the confidence to solve their own problems?

Underlying our temptation to give solutions is a feeling that "good teachers" or "good parents" are supposed to lift problems off their charges' shoulders. But, when we do for others what they (if given the chance) can do for themselves, we hurt them, rather than help them. When someone asks for your opinion, your solution, do not be so ready to give it. The person with the problem who says, "What do you think I should do?" or "What would you do in my place?" may not really want you to answer. Often, such statements are just an awkward way of ending, for the moment, what they have to say and turning the dialogue over to you, the listener. Don't respond by telling them what you would do in their situation. You are not in their situation!

Further, responding with a solution to their problem assumes that the words they have used adequately reveal the real, often underlying, problem they are facing. Often the real problem does not surface until much later in the dialogue. For instance, when a person says, "I am so mad at him I could kill him," do we really believe his words? Do we actually think he is contemplating murder? Or, do we take his words as simply a signal of some other problem that has not been revealed?

Another Roadblock is Probing, Questioning, Interrogating. Although Probing and Interrogating seem inherently inappropriate, what could be wrong with Questioning? The moment you ask a question, the person who owns the problem must typically answer your question. This is especially true in schools where students have been conditioned to answer when teachers ask. By asking questions, you take control of the conversation. Chances are, once started, you will ask questions until you have enough information to offer your solution. Note the number of references to "you(r)" in the preceding sentence. Can parents and teachers know just the right question to ask out of the thousands that could be asked? How are they able to select that question based on just a sentence or two from the person who owns the problem? Even trained clinical psychologists would not act on such little information.

Finally, Analyzing and Diagnosing is another Roadblock to Communication when a teacher responds to a student who owns a problem. This is a Catch-22 situation. If the teacher's diagnosis is incorrect, the student feels as if the teacher has not really listened at all. If the diagnosis is correct, the student may feel exposed, feel naked. He may not be ready to handle the fact that someone else has him figured out even before he, himself, does.

ALTERNATIVES TO ROADBLOCKS

At this point some readers may feel a little guilty, for it is all too easy to remember times when we have delivered Roadblocks to Communication. But, if not Roadblocks, what then? Gordon suggests Silence, Noncommittal Responses, Door-Openers, and finally, Active Listening.

To keep communication lines open, often attentive Silence works. Body posture and eye contact show the person with the problem that you are tuned in, yet Silence leaves the responsibility to continue with him. The pressure, and at the same time respect, that Silence displays conveys a faith in the other person's own problem-solving ability.

Noncommittal Responses are simply "grunts" of one sort or another that, properly delivered, convey that the listener is not only tuned in to the sender's problem, but tuned in to the intensity of the problem. "Oh," "My gosh," "You don't say," "I see," and "No fooling" are all powerful ways to interact with a sender and, at the same time, avoid any Roadblocks to Communication. Demonstrating that one is in tune with the intensity of the sender's feelings is highlighted by selecting the proper Noncommittal Response. A response such as "No fooling" may be appropriate for a child who tells you he got drenched on the way to school, but inappropriate in intensity for the high school student who sobs out the story that she just did very poorly on her College Board Exams.

Door-Openers are fairly straightforward. "Do you want to talk about it?" and "Let's hear more what you have to say," convey a message to the sender that you are ready and willing to listen to whatever he wants to say about his problem. If he chooses not to talk, so be it. It is his problem; he has the right to talk about it or not talk about it. If he doesn't take you up on your offer, have you failed him? I think not. What you have done with the Door-Opener is let him know that you are ready now, and you are probably the kind of person who will be ready in the future, to listen to him. Even a Door-Opener that is not taken advantage of when given sets a positive foundation for the future.

Active Listening is even more effective than Silence, Noncommittal Responses, or Door-Openers. It is, in theory, the same as Carl Rogers' Reflective Listening—listening to the client (student) and mirroring the message and THE FEELINGS behind the message for his immediate confirmation. If this form of response seems unusual, remember that it is not at all uncommon for people seeking professional help with their personal problems to pay hard-earned money to a counselor who does little else but listen! Listening, especially Active Listening, is therapeutic.

Often an active listener would start a response by saying, "It sounds as if you . . . ," "I sense that you are feeling . . . ," "I hear you say-ing. . . ." The inflection at the end of each response should convey, "Am I hearing you correctly?" In each case the sender, the person with the problem, has the chance to affirm or disaffirm the listener's attempt to decode his message. The sender might say, "Yes, that's exactly how I feel," or "No, it's not that, it's more like. . . ."

What might be appropriate responses to the two situations identified earlier (Mr. Gamble and Eileen) where it was clear they owned a problem and you wanted to help?

> #1 "Mr. Gamble, you really seem to be upset today. Do you want to talk about it?" Just think how tempting it would be to send one or more of the Roadblocks to Communication. For example, "I know just how you feel" (Consoling); "You are just feeling upset be-cause you had an argument with the principal" (Diagnosing); "I think you are one of the best teachers in the school" (Praising); "Why don't we forget about it and have a cup of coffee?" (With-drawing).
>
> #2 "If I hear you correctly, Eileen, you feel pretty frustrated with today's mathematics assignment. Is that right?" (*Note,* I did not tell her she WAS frustrated. I asked her if that is how SHE thinks SHE feels.)

Each of these alternative responses is designed to keep the lines of communication open. Each conveys faith that the individual with the problem is the best person to solve, or at least *handle the feelings* asso-ciated with, the problem.

The words "handle the feelings" point out the reality of our world, where many student (as well as adult) problems cannot be solved. At best, only the debilitating feelings associated with the problem can be handled. A fellow teacher's spouse becomes ill, a child's parent is suddenly unem-ployed, a student is not selected to his first-choice university, all are problems without immediate solutions. Yet, the feelings about the problem are still there. Here is where Active Listening shines.

Do these two Active Listening responses seem too artificial or too clinical? I believe they will not seem that way to the person who is knee-deep in a problem. For a moment, put yourself in Mr. Gamble's and Eileen's place. Haven't each of the Active Listening statements above left the door open for you to talk more about your problem IF YOU WANT TO? When used in a real situation where the owner of the problem is looking for a listener, wouldn't each of these statements convey a degree of trust and confidence in your ability to solve your problem?

Finally, teachers can also actively listen to students who have positive problems—William just found out that he did considerably better on his SATs than expected; Susan just passed that dreaded calculus exam. Both have to tell someone the great news. Once again, until the feelings, positive or negative, are handled, little learning will take place.

I-MESSAGES: WHEN YOU OWN A PROBLEM

What skill does Gordon recommend using when you, the teacher, own the problem? My professional training, first as a classroom teacher and then as a guidance counselor, stressed what I should do to serve the needs of my students who "owned problems." After several years of teaching and counseling, I wondered what I was supposed to do when "I owned a problem." How could I get my needs met? I found the answer in Gordon's Effectiveness Training model. It has a set of responding skills not only to help me to help others who "owned problems," but also to help me when "I owned a problem."

When "I own the problem," I have looked through Gordon's window/rectangle, classified the other person's behavior as being "unacceptable" (interfering with my meeting my needs), and recognized the need to confront the other person in order to get him to stop his behavior. How one confronts another person can be the key to getting your needs met.

For those who have power over others who cause them a problem, too often their answer is to MAKE others alter their behavior. When others interfere with our needs, it is tempting to send power-based messages. Gordon calls these You-Messages. "You stop that talking while I am teaching or else!" "If you know what is good for you, you will stop acting like a cry-baby and start cleaning up the garage." One can picture the teacher (or parent) shaking his finger at the "other" person while uttering these messages. Perhaps it is obvious, but it bears saying: You-Messages incorporate one or more of Gordon's twelve Roadblocks to Communication. Among others, they send solutions (yours), they moralize, they lecture, they ridicule, they threaten, or, as in the sentences above, they may do several of these at one time. They also close off communication!

But don't teachers (and others in power) have the right to bark the kinds of commands shown above? Perhaps they do; but should they? You-Messages may force the other person to alter his behavior, but at what cost? They often result in defiant compliance, cause the other person to lose face, and weaken the relationship between the two of you—after all, you have won, and he has lost. Why take this chance when an alternative to You-Messages, I-Messages, exists.

A properly constructed I-Message consists of three parts: a nonblameful description of the other person's behavior that is interfering with your meeting your needs, the tangible effect now or in the future that that behavior is having on you, and the feeling that tangible effect is causing you. Below are two situations where, as a teacher, you might judge the student behaviors to be "unacceptable." Immediately following each situation is an I-Message designed to confront the student, get him to willingly change his behavior, allow both to save face, and to do as little damage as possible to the relationship.

#1 John, an eager third grade student of yours, continually blurts out answers before being formally called upon. The effect of his behavior is that no one else has an opportunity to answer, and you are not sure the other students are following your lesson.

I-Message: "John, when you call out the answers before I have had a chance to call on other students, I am not sure the whole class knows the material. As a result, I may not be doing as good a job as your parents pay me to do."

#2 Before leaving school, you rearrange the students' desks into a semicircle in preparation for a theatre exercise you plan to do first thing the next morning. You write a note asking that the pattern of the desks be left untouched. The next day you come in only to find that the custodian has put the desks back into a straight-row pattern.

I-Message: "When you ignore my note asking that you leave the student desks in their semicircle pattern and, instead, place them back into straight rows, I must take time at the beginning of class to rearrange them. As a result, I feel really pressured by not having enough time adequately to present my theatre exercise."

From the teacher's point of view it would be tempting to send a You-Message such as, in the first example, "John, stop trying to show everyone how smart you are" (Diagnosing); "John, a good little boy would raise his hand and wait to be called" (Moralizing); or "If you blurt out the answer one more time without raising your hand, you are in real trouble" (Threatening).

Each of the alternative I-Messages contains the necessary three parts. In reference to John who blurts out answers, the first sentence of the I-Message points out the behavior that is interfering with the teacher's meeting her needs. The next part describes the tangible effect the behavior is having on the teacher. The second sentence describes the teacher's feelings.

An I-Message does not tell the other person how he should change his behavior. That is left up to him. He has a chance to change his behavior voluntarily. Further, an I-Message does not say anything about the other person; it concentrates only upon you. I-Messages tell how "you" are being tangibly affected and tell how "you" feel. Unlike You-Messages, where the other person is likely to dig in his heels and resist or fight back, it is pretty hard for the other person to get defensive when the focus of the I-Message is not on him. An I-Message conveys, as does Active Listening, a trust in the other person. It says that our relationship is strong enough that if I lay out for you what you are doing that interferes with my meeting my needs, you will more than likely volunteer to alter your behavior.

On the outside chance that the other person would get defensive when an I-Message is sent, you have a skill to help handle the problem he now feels he has. That skill is Active Listening. After using Active Listening to defuse his defensive feelings, the teacher would once again present his I-Message.

No doubt some teachers are skeptical about exposing their feelings so openly to a student. I-Messages require a teacher to be honest with students and acknowledge that they (students) do have the power through their behaviors to interfere with teachers meeting their own needs. This is the "tangible effect" portion of the message. When one adds admitting true human feelings such as fear, discouragement, frustration, or vulnerability, the "feelings" portion of the message, this may take more courage and trust than some teachers possess. To these doubters I respond by saying that there is one other very strong reason why I-Messages work so well. If, as a teacher, parent, boss, spouse, or good friend, you have helped others by Active Listening when they had problems, I believe they will be looking for opportunities to reciprocate — to pay you back. They will want to help you as they feel you have helped them. Your I-Message gives others the opportunity to respond by altering their behavior so that you may get your needs met.

I-Messages work on the assumption that you and the other person have an ongoing relationship — one that has basically been beneficial to both of you. Teachers need students, and students need teachers. Further, it is assumed that as a teacher you probably have had opportunities to use Active Listening with one or more of the students to whom you are sending your I-Message. Thus, they have a reason to reciprocate your earlier helping behaviors. Often they will say, "Gee, I'm sorry. I didn't realize that it was affecting you, how about if I . . . ? Remember, the alternative to an I-Message is a finger-shaking You-Message.

Most people use I-Messages on others who possess equal power, realizing that they are not in a position to enforce the demands of a You-Message. Almost by default and, it seems to me somewhat reluctantly, I-Messages are used when You-Messages are perceived to be ineffective. Gordon suggests that we not wait until we have no choice but to use I-Messages. I agree.

DON'T KEEP T.E.T. A SECRET

Tell your students that you value your relationship with them and, as a result, have decided to use some skills that should enhance that relationship. Explain at an appropriate level for the audience (for example, elementary or high school) the philosophy behind Gordon's model—trust and faith in the other person. Explain the fundamentals of Active Listening and I-Messages. Acknowledge that you may sound a little phoney when you first practice these skills, but because of the value you place on strengthening your relationship, you feel it is worth it. Gordon's Effectiveness Training model and the skills contained within work best when both parties are informed. In this way no one feels that something is being "used on them."

A significant side benefit of using the T.E.T. skills on others is that through modeling they, too, may start to use it as their vehicle for problem solving. Just imagine the decrease in discipline problems in schools if students would use Active Listening and I-Messages on each other. For instance, it is a fact that students are going to confront each other, with or without the knowledge of Gordon's communication model—for that matter, so are teachers and administrators. Remember, the alternative of an I-Message is a less desirable and less effective power-based You-Message.

Having once taught physics and mathematics at the comprehensive school level, I thought my greatest achievement as a teacher would be to have graduated students knowledgeable of such material as Newton's Laws and quadratic equations. In hindsight, although this subject-specific information is certainly important, if I had to choose with what knowledge and skills students left school, I would choose communication skills. Such skills promote the most effective discipline—self-discipline—in school as well as in society. Until something better comes along, the communication model I would use would be Gordon's.

SUMMARY

Do Active Listening and I-Messages work all the time? The answer is definitely "No!" Human interaction is not an exact science. We are playing the odds, looking for those skills that work with most people, in most situations, most of the time. Active Listening works better than Roadblocks to Communication. I-Messages work better than You-Messages. Both are effective skills to keep the lines of communication open between a teacher and a student or, for that matter, between any two people. Active Listening and I-Messages are based on mutual trust and respect—the foundation for any strong and lasting relationship.

REFERENCES

Gordon, T. (1970). *Parent effectiveness training.* New York: Peter H. Wyden, Inc.

Gordon, T. (1974). *Teacher effectiveness training.* New York: Peter H.
Wyden, Inc.
Gordon, T. (1977). *Leader effectiveness training.* New York: Bantam
Books, Inc.

Note: For a discussion of "Praise" as one of Gordon's Roadblocks to Communication, see:
Tauber, R. (1986). The positive side of negative reinforcement and the negative
side of praise. *The Durham and Newcastle RESEARCH REVIEW, 10*(56), 299–302.
No EJ number cited.

FURTHER READINGS RELATED TO GORDON'S MODEL

Chanow-Gruen, K., & Doyle, R. (1983). The counselor's consultative role
with teachers, using the TET Model. *Humanistic Education and
Development, 22*(1), 16–24. EJ 286-436.
Cleveland, B. (1980). Active listening yields better discussion. *The Social
Studies, 71*(5), 218–221. EJ 235-207.
Clifton, D., & Cottrell, V. (1975). T.E.T. teacher effectiveness training/
Gordon. *NASSP Bulletin, 59*(388), 75–76. EJ 111- 965.
Gordon, T. (1981). Crippling our children with discipline. *Journal of
Education, 163*(3), 228–243. EJ 254-581.
McWhirter, J., & Kahn, S. (1974). A parent communication group. *Ele-
mentary School Guidance and Counseling, 9*(2), 116–122. EJ 108-937.
Nummela, R., & Avila, D. (1980). Self-concept and teacher effectiveness
training. *College Student Journal, 14*(3), 314–316. EJ 233-848.
Peterson, B. (1971). The teacher effectiveness program. *Journal of the
Student Personnel Association for Teacher Education, 9*(3), 71–75.
EJ 038-104.
Pinsker, M., & Geoffroy, K. (1981). A comparison of parent effectiveness
training and behavior modification parent training. *Family Relations,
30*(1), 61–68. EJ 239-974.
Wiseman, D., & Puskar, E. (1976). The teacher-to-teacher communication
gap: Not a hopeless case. *College Student Journal, 10*(3), 265–268.
EJ 146-112.

Note: The EJ number (for example, EJ 306-689) that follows each journal article can be used,
in conjunction with the ERIC system described in Chapter IV, to obtain a copy of
that article.

DREIKURS'S GOALS OF MISBEHAVIOR
Recognition of Student Goals: A Prerequisite to Reacting

INTRODUCTION

According to Dreikurs, children are social beings. They have a need to
know that they belong. They want evidence that they are significant. They

seek recognition. Is this too much to ask? I think not. The problem occurs, though, when children are unable to achieve these goals through socially accepted means; they may well resort to antisocial means.

When students operate under the mistaken belief that misbehaving will gain them recognition and status, teachers must take action. But what action? As a practical matter, teachers should not, in fact cannot, decide what action to take until they first identify which goal misbehaving students are seeking.

Dreikurs identifies four goals which describe the purpose of children's misbehavior. They include, in a sequence from least serious to most serious:

- Bids for Attention
- Power Struggles
- Revenge Seeking
- Displays of Inadequacy

Misbehaving children will engage in purposeful (goal-directed) behavior designed to achieve one or more of these goals. If bids for attention are unsuccessful in reassuring the child that he belongs, he may well resort to more serious tactics—for example, revenge seeking, displays of inadequacy. Teachers would be well warned to deal with misbehaving children while they are seeking one of the less serious goals—for example, bids for attention and power struggles.

How can teachers tell which goal of misbehavior a student is seeking? Dreikurs describes several distinct clues teachers can use to help them decide a child's goal. Two of these three clues deal with the teacher's examining himself—his feelings *and* his previous efforts at correcting the child's misbehavior.

CLUES TO A CHILD'S GOAL FOR MISBEHAVING

1. How do you feel when the child displays the misbehavior?
2. How have you typically responded to the child's misbehavior?
3. How has the child responded to your attempts at correction?

Clue #1: Teacher's Feelings

Teachers typically feel ANNOYED when a student is making a constant bid for their attention. Like a gnat that is always in their face, they wish the child would go away and stop bothering them. When a child is engaged in a power struggle, teachers feel their authority has been THREATENED. They feel ANGRY. They feel a need to pull the child down off his high horse and SHOW HIM WHO IS BOSS. A feeling of HURT accompanies situations where a student is seeking revenge. Teachers feel, *how could this child have done this to me?* Finally, teachers feel a sense of DESPAIR and HELPLESSNESS when a child is displaying inadequacy. The point is to take a moment before acting and ask, "How am I feeling right now while the child is misbehaving?" An honest answer can go a long way toward identifying the child's goal of misbehavior.

Clue #2: Teacher's Typical Response to a Child's Misbehavior

When a child is making a bid for attention, it is common for teachers to REMIND and COAX. They might remind a child twenty times a week that he is to raise his hand before calling out an answer. For a child who finds himself in a power struggle with teachers, too often teachers resort to FIGHTING BACK or GIVING IN. "No student of mine is going to get away with such and such," or "Why bother, what's the use, I may as well look the other way and give in." Where a child appears to be seeking revenge, teachers may well RETALIATE in an effort to get even or settle the score. Finally, teachers are often overheard to say, "I've tried everything with this student, I give up," when a child is displaying inadequacy.

These typical teacher responses to a student's misbehavior, in most cases, simply make matters worse. Reminding and coaxing only lead to more reminding and coaxing. Fighting back or giving in results in an unproductive and unhealthy win-lose or lose-win situation. Retaliating only confirms to the child that his initial efforts at revenge were justified — "See everyone is out to get me, look at what the teacher just did." Giving up on a student only helps confirm his or her inadequacy.

Clue #3: Child's Response to Teacher's Corrective Efforts

When a child is making a bid for attention, reminding and coaxing seem to work — but only temporarily. The child stops the unwanted behavior only to resume it or another unwanted behavior soon afterwards. The reason for this is that reminding and coaxing in no way help to make the child more responsible or more independent. In fact, these typical teacher responses do just the opposite — they make the child less responsible and more dependent. Remember, too, that the student's bid for attention is his mistaken way of trying to belong and be recognized. Belonging is a basic deficiency need as described by Maslow. It is episodic. Just like eating and breathing, it is a need that must continually be replenished. The reader may wish to review the article in Chapter III, "Maslow's Hierarchy."

For those children who find themselves in a power struggle with the teacher, fighting back only results in an escalation or intensification of the struggle. If the student complies at all, it is done so defiantly. Misbehaving children are discouraged — their inappropriate behavior is a last resort to belong and gain status. Pulling a child down off his high horse or cutting him down to size and showing him who is boss by fighting back only increases his discouragement. On the other hand, if a teacher responds by giving in, then students are sent clear, but unintended messages—their needs come first, they can be boss, no one can make them do anything they don't want to do. The reader may wish to review the article in Chapter III, "Defusing Power Struggles."

If a teacher responds with an eye-for-an-eye, revenge-for-revenge strategy, one can expect children to do likewise. Like a snowball rolling down a hill, getting bigger and bigger, where will it ever end? It is not uncommon for students seeking revenge not only to become violent or hostile, but to feel justified in doing so. Before the teacher actually retaliated, the student *only thought* others were out to hurt him. When a teacher falls into the trap of actually retaliating, the student *has* concrete evidence that others are out to get him!

Passive response or failure to respond at all can be expected of children who have teachers who throw their hands up in despair and give up. It is all too easy for a teacher, in her frustration, to "take the picture of him as a student worth teaching out of her picture album" (Glasser 1986, p. 53). Having teachers give up on a child confirms to him that he is incapable of doing anything—just what he mistakenly thought in the beginning. Now he has his teachers agreeing with him. He thinks, "Both of us can't be wrong. I must, in fact, be inadequate." Remaining passive and doing nothing enables students to guard what little self-esteem they have left by removing it from social tests (Charles 1985, p. 76).

Recognition Reflex — A Final Clue

After examining your feelings while the child is misbehaving (noting how you have typically responded in the past, and looking at how the misbehaving child has reacted to your responses), you are in a good position to judge which of Dreikurs' four goals of misbehavior the child is seeking. One final "litmus test" is to confront the child with a statement that represents that goal of misbehavior and look for a recognition reflex.

Where possible, the teacher should first ask the child why he misbehaved. Taken out of context, literally "asking a child why he misbehaved" violates the suggestion in Chapter II of "Don't Ask Why" and violates one of the points made in the Chapter III article, "Glasser's Reality Therapy." Dreikurs knows that a child can't answer this question. The real point of the question is to set the stage for the teacher then to say, "May I tell you what I think?"

The four confrontation statements are:

1. "Could it be that you would like to keep me busy with you?"
2. "Could it be that you would like to be boss and show everyone that no one can make you do anything?"
3. "Could it be that you would like to hurt others as you think they have hurt you?"
4. "Could it be that you would like to convince others that you are not capable?"

How long will it take, and what, exactly, is a recognition reflex? According to Dreikurs, Grunwald, and Pepper (1971, p. 41):

> The recognition reflex may not come immediately because the child may have to think it over first. Therefore, one has to wait for his reaction. It is most dramatic to watch the child, how he first considers it, and then the corners of his mouth begin to expand in a knowing smile and a gleam appears in his eyes. He begins to recognize what he was up to.

With the child's goal now out in the open for both the child and the teacher to see, real progress can be made. Teachers can now respond in ways more likely *not* to reinforce the mistaken goals of misbehavior. Keep in mind that in the world of operant learning, "not reinforcing" is the way, the only way, to extinguish an unwanted behavior.

ALTERNATIVE BEHAVIORS FOR TEACHERS

Once a teacher has determined a child's goal of misbehavior, corrective responses can be made. Alternative responses to each goal of misbehavior are described below.

Bids for Attention

Teachers should ignore a student's bid for attention, where possible, *and* give attention to positive behavior when the student is not making a bid for it. Student misbehavior that threatens to cause harm to him, to fellow students, or to the environment, of course, cannot be ignored. But, much of the type of misbehavior that teachers find ANNOYING (Dreikurs's signal for students making a bid for attention) can be ignored.

However, ignoring alone is ineffective because it only results in the student's either escalating his misbehavior, or moving to examples of more serious misbehavior—power struggles, and so on. Keep in mind that the student's bid for attention is a goal-directed behavior. Ignoring that behavior interferes with the child's achieving his goal. On the other hand, supplying attention when the child is not making a bid for it reinforces the cause-and-effect relationship between engaging in acceptable behavior and receiving attention. The student soon realizes that if he does his work, obeys the social norms (rules), and so on, he will receive evidence that he is accepted, belongs, and is recognized.

Something else occurs when a student sets to work, believing that in doing so he will receive the attention he seeks. The more he learns whatever it is he is to learn, the more he gains in confidence, the better he does on tests, and the more he feels the master of his own fate. Internal motivation starts to replace external motivation. Locus of control shifts from without to within. As a result, the student needs less and less of the teacher's overt attention, for now he is better able to get the same feelings of worth and recognition through his own achievements.

Power Struggles

As stated earlier, fighting back or giving in simply does not work. Both are win-lose situations. Teachers should disengage from a power struggle. Just as it takes "two to tango," it takes "two to tangle." The steam quickly goes out of a power struggle when a student finds himself trying to sustain a power struggle when there is not one to struggle with.

Part of disengaging from a power struggle is to help the child understand the goal of his misbehavior (for example, his need to be boss). According to Dreikurs, Grunwald, and Pepper (1971, p. 199), this "removes from him the conviction that he is just a bad child, and opens avenues for alternatives."

Just as it was ineffective simply to ignore a student's bid for attention, it is equally ineffective simply to withdraw from a power struggle. A teacher must do more. Remember, the child's behaviors are goal-directed. Withdrawing from the power struggle leaves that goal unattained. Teachers must redirect the student's need for power into constructive endeavors. But how does a teacher do this?

Admitting to a child that you don't know what to do about his misbehavior *and then* asking him, "What do you think we can do to solve the problem," gives the misbehaving student a prosocial opportunity (and responsibility) to "be the boss." Who knows, as a teacher you may well be surprised with the quality of solutions generated. As is the case in "Glasser's Reality Therapy" (Chapter III, p. 130), corrective plans generated by a student should only be accepted if they meet the teacher's need. Further, does it really matter who comes up with a solution to the problem behavior as long as the problem is solved?

Admitting to students that you cannot make them complete a particular assignment, or force them to turn in such and such paper IF THEY DO NOT WANT TO, acknowledges the fact that they, and only they, have the final power over their behavior. Students know this to be true, and by your saying so, students know you know it to be true. Once out in the open, students have less of a need to continue trying to prove it to be so. The fact is, the incomplete assignment or nonsubmitted paper is a smoke screen to hide the student's feeling of powerlessness. Often students act "big" to conceal just how "small" or discouraged they really feel.

There are so few people in this world who want to take on the responsibilities of being the boss or the leader, why not capitalize upon those students who do? Assign them "posts of responsibility." Let them be lunch monitor, take messages to the office, help younger children, oversee the distribution of materials, be a crossing guard, and so on. Most people, including children, take assignments of responsibility, of power, quite seriously. After all, by doing so they are getting their needs for power, for status, for recognition, met. At the same time, they are going about it in a socially acceptable way.

Revenge Seeking

The first piece of advice is "Don't retaliate" and "Don't take it personally." Although the student's behavior is goal-directed, it is not normally directed at you, in particular. The child is striking out—you just happen to be there. As difficult as it may be, teachers must show that they care for the student and for his or her well-being.

I am reminded of the situation where a teenager says to a parent, "I hate you, I wish you were not my parent!" These are razor-sharp hurting words. The urge to retaliate is great. Think what it does, though, when the parent responds by saying, "Well, I still love you."

If the child's goal of misbehavior is acknowledged (for example, "Could it be that you want to hurt others as much as you believe they have hurt you?") and then followed by sincere caring statements *and* caring actions, there will be less and less of a need for the student to continue seeking revenge. Once students begin to believe that they belong, there is little motivation to continue acts of revenge against others (teacher, peers, and so on). To do so would undo their sense of belonging, their sense of recognition.

Displays of Inadequacy

When a child exhibits displays of inadequacy, find something the child CAN do, and at which he CAN succeed. Focus on the child's assets. Statements such as "I know you have it in you," and "I really believe you can do it," can help create the motivation and initiative to start the child trying. Once the child is making an attempt, any attempt, the opportunity then exists for the teacher to offer tons and tons of encouragement.

Eventually you will want to wean the child from all of this external encouragement and praise. But for now, load it on. If you don't begin to convince him that he is a capable person who is going to? According to Balson (1982, pp. 72–73), these children "need positive reassurance by teachers of their worth and ability so they can begin to function usefully, constructively and co-operatively."

REFERENCES

Balson, M. (1982). *Understanding classroom behavior.* Hawthorne, Victoria: The Australian Council for Educational Research Limited.

Charles, C. (1985). *Building classroom discipline.* White Plains, NY: Longman, Inc.

Dreikurs, R., Grunwald, B., & Pepper, F. (1971). *Maintaining sanity in the classroom: Illustrated teaching techniques.* New York: Harper & Row.

Glasser, W. (1986). *Control theory in the classroom.* New York: Harper & Row.

GLASSER'S REALITY THERAPY
Students Take Responsibility for Forming a Plan to Stop Their Own Misbehavior — It Really Works!

INTRODUCTION

About the time I was writing this article, I met with a principal to ask him to review a draft of this book. He mentioned that two weeks earlier he had traveled to New York where he observed a school in which all the teachers had been trained in Glasser's model. To put it mildly, he was impressed. Hearing him say this reinforced two ideas of mine. One, no book on classroom management would be complete without Glasser. Two, as stressed in Chapter I, there is little brand new in the world of discipline — Glasser's theories are as applicable now as they were two decades ago.

This article will describe Glasser's model — his prerequisites that school be a good and fair place (rule formation) and the steps in his Reality Therapy. These steps include: securing student involvement, identifying problem behavior, evaluating inappropriate behavior, planning new behavior, gaining commitment, accepting no excuses, and avoiding punishment. The article will also describe the heavy, but appropriate, responsibility students are asked to assume in this model.

School Must Be a Good Place

Before any classroom management strategy can be expected to succeed, students must first perceive school as a good place to be. For instance, the strategy of supplying time-out (for example, in-school suspension, removing students from the classroom and placing them out in the hall), or the removal of the child from a rewarding situation works only if the child perceives his school and/or his classroom experience to be rewarding. In other words, the strategies work if he sees his school, his classroom, as a good place to be.

The same holds for Glasser's model. In Glasser's model there is a shared responsibility between the teacher and the student. This acceptance of responsibility by students is far more likely to occur if they perceive school as a good place. Increased student choice is an outcome of increased student responsibility. Schools that are a "good place to be," are, in fact, schools where students would normally choose to be, given alternatives. They are getting their needs met. According to Gough (1987, p. 658), "discipline problems do not occur in classrooms in which students' needs are satisfied."

Once students have chosen to be there, they have a stake in making there, the school, an even better place to be. Students have less motivation to misbehave; there is less need for teachers to use strategies of classroom management.

What makes school a good place? "A good school could be defined as a place where almost all students believe that if they do some work, they will be able to satisfy their needs enough so that it makes sense to keep working" (Glasser 1986, p. 15). It is one where students believe they are important and they have power—both of which lead to increased self-esteem (Brandt 1988, p. 39). More specifically, Glasser (1977, p. 61) describes a good school as a place where:

> People are courteous, especially the adults.
> One frequently hears laughter that springs from genuine joy brought about by involvement with caring people engaged in relevant work.
> Communication is *practiced* and not just *preached*. People talk with, not at, each other.
> Reasonable rules, recognized to be beneficial to both the individual and the group, exist.
> Administrators actively support and participate in an approach to discipline that teaches self-responsibility.

Of the criteria listed above for making schools a good place, the one referring to reasonable rules deserves further elaboration. It deserves further attention because it is the one criterion educators can best tangibly use to share the responsibility for solving problem behaviors. Reasonable rules do not just happen, they come about as a result of reasonable people using reason. The process of forming reasonable rules is as important as the reasonable rules that emerge. The process, as Glasser views it, is one of involving both students and teachers. This involvement goes a long way to demonstrate the need for problems that affect both students and the teacher to have solutions that involve both students and the teacher.

Specifically, what does Glasser say about rules? First and foremost he states, "Reasonable rules, firmly enforced through separation from the program (not punishment) . . . are a necessary part of helping students become responsible enough to take advantage of what is made available to them" (Glasser 1969, p. 194). He believes that students should know the rules. Although, in fact, ignorance of the law (rules) is no excuse for breaking the law, there is little to be lost and lots to be gained by clearly displaying the school rules. And, because sharing the school rules is so easy to do, it would be a shame if problem behaviors occurred simply because the student did not know his or her action was against the rules. Copies of the rules can be passed out, can be included in student handbooks, can be sent home to be shared with parents, can be displayed in individual classrooms, and so on.

Within reason, students should agree with the rules. The more reasonable the rule, the more likely the student will agree with it. What determines whether or not a rule is reasonable? Reasonable rules are those in which cause and effect relationships are clear. Walking in the halls (cause) is more likely to have students arrive safely to their next class (effect). On the other hand, running in the halls (cause) is more likely to result in accidents (effect). Such cause and effect relationships can easily be identified regarding throwing things, hitting other people, taking turns to talk in class, and so on.

In fact, *IF* you cannot show the existence of a cause and effect relationship for a rule, I would question the need for the rule in the first place! Without the logic of a cause and effect relationship, rules appear capricious, dictatorial, and unreasonable. Woe to the teacher or administrator who tries to make students obey unreasonable rules. One would be doomed before one started. Further, in Glasser's model, unreasonable anything—including rules—would interfere with students' believing schools are good places to be.

There will be those cases where, in spite of explaining the cause and effect reason for a rule, some students still will not agree with it. So be it. You can do little more. Chances are that reasonable rules will prevail. Peer pressure, the masses of students convinced by the explained logic of the rules, will help convince some holdouts.

Students should also play a role in both forming the rules and, when necessary, changing the rules. Although it may be more expedient for teachers simply to form the rules themselves, type them, and distribute them, Glasser would suggest one do otherwise. There is no doubt that students who have part "ownership" in a rule have more incentive to follow the rule. Ownership is obtained by helping to form the rules in the first place.

As an assignment, education majors of mine who are placed in sophomore-level field experiences in local schools ask their elementary students to participate in forming five or six rules that would help the classroom run more smoothly. Sure as shooting, these students come up with almost exactly the same rules that the teacher would have formed if she had created them herself! "Walk, don't run," "One person talks at a time," "Keeping one's hands to one's self," and "Being quiet when the teacher talks to another adult" are common favorites.

I understand that these elementary students are the products of their prior years in school, complete with dictated rules, and, as such, would be expected to veer little in their rule formation. Still, when students help form the classroom rules, they do experience some degree of ownership. The rules are now partially their rules. Who wants to break something of their own? Not me. Not students. See the Chapter II suggestion, "*R* for Rules and Procedures," for further information on rules.

Selling Reality Therapy

Glasser's model, called Reality Therapy, carries more information than may meet the eye. Reality Therapy does not deal with a psychoanalytic-based approach to problem behaviors. Glasser is less interested in the reasons found in a child's past that might explain his problem behaviors than he is in having the child deal with the here and now — reality. The reality of a child's life, in or out of school, is that the present, not the past, is where he can make choices. He cannot do anything about his past; it is gone forever.

On the other hand, he can do something about his future, a point in his life influenced by his present choices. As a rational being, he can make tomorrow what he wants it to be — it depends upon the behaviors he chooses now. Through a clearly defined set of steps, teachers can use Glasser's Reality Therapy to help create the facilitative and supportive environment necessary for children to embark upon a path of assuming increased responsibility for their own lives.

Glasser believes students are rational beings — they choose their behaviors. They can choose to be good, and they can choose to be bad. Teachers need to structure the environment in order to help students make better choices. The steps in Reality Therapy provide this structure.

Steps in Reality Therapy

The steps in Reality Therapy read somewhat like a recipe in a cookbook. Do not expect the finished product, improved student behavior, to turn out as it is supposed to unless all the steps in the recipe are followed. The steps in Reality Therapy include:

1. Secure Student Involvement — Be Personal. When school is seen as a good place, a place where, among other things, teachers display warmth and caring behavior toward students, such involvement is relatively easy to achieve. See the Chapter II suggestion, "*C* for Caring for Students *and* Showing It."

2. Identify the Problem Behavior. The mutual trust and personal involvement begun in step one are continued in this step, when the teacher asks a student to identify his own misbehavior. Although it would be more expedient for the teacher simply to tell the student what he has done wrong, this would rob him of the chance to take responsibility for his behaviors.

   Deal only with the present, not with the past. Simply ask, in as caring a manner as possible, "John, what are you doing?" If he tries to distract you by telling what someone else did, say, "John, at this point I do not want to know what so-and-so did. I want to know what *you* are doing." Keep at this question, even at the expense of sounding like a broken record. Avoid bringing up John's history of past sins — his "rap record." Don't encourage John to give excuses for his misbehavior by asking him "Why" he misbehaved. See the Chapter II suggestion, "*Y* for Don't Ask *Why*," for more information on this point.

   If it sounds incredible to expect a student to admit what he has done wrong, keep in mind two points. First, you have already set the stage for cooperation in step one by securing student involvement. Second, the main reason students avoid owning up to their misbehavior is fear that they will be punished. The last step in Reality Therapy, "Avoiding Punishment," removes this road-block to honesty.

3. Call for Value Judgments. It would, of course, also be more expedient for the teacher to judge the misbehavior and tell the student exactly why his behavior is bad for him. To do so, would be counterproductive to having the student assume greater responsibility for his actions.

The judgment sought in this step is a cause and effect one, not a moral one. A student who is caught copying homework (cause) will not learn the material (effect). A child who constantly bothers other children in the classroom (cause) will interfere with their ability to study (effect). A student who throws stones on the playground (cause) may cause a serious injury (effect). One's misbehavior is just that—behavior. It is behavior that one chooses to display *and* that one can choose not to display.

Moral judgments, on the other hand, connect a child's misbehavior to something about his character as a human being—something most of us find difficult to change. A student who is caught copying homework is labeled a "cheat"; a child who constantly bothers others is labeled as "lacking self control"; a child who throws stones on the playground is labeled "a bully or troublemaker."

Once the student understands the cause and effect relationship between what he is doing and what is happening as a result of what he has done, he is better able to come up with a concrete plan, Glasser's step four, for changing his behavior. Most important of all, the more practice a student has in evaluating his own behavior, the more likely he is to internalize the value of changing his behavior. It is this act of internalizing that equips the student with the commitment to make the change in behavior more lasting (Raffini 1980, p. 103).

4. Plan a New Behavior. By now, the strategy is clear—let the student assume the primary responsibility for his misbehavior *and* for developing a plan to change that behavior. The teacher might ask, "Susan, what is your plan to make sure that this misbehavior does not occur in the future?" For those new to the responsibility of planning new behaviors, a teacher might suggest a couple of plans, and then leave it to the student to either choose one of them or choose an original plan of his/her own. The key is that students are choosing; they are starting to take responsibility.

As a student gains experience in planning new behaviors, the teacher will less often have to make suggestions. With the experience comes the confidence. With the experience and confidence comes an increased feeling of responsibility over one's life. Students make more and more good choices of behavior and fewer and fewer bad choices of behavior.

Occasionally a student will come along who you believe is simply unwilling to take the responsibility for planning new behaviors. He might respond to your request to do so by saying, "I can't think of a plan." The temptation might be to give him one of your plans and get the problem behavior settled. Don't give in to temptation. Instead, put the student in a time-out situation (for example, a safe, comfortable, but rather sterile corner of the room), and tell him that he will remain there until he does formulate a plan. When he comes up with a plan, acceptable to both of you, he can rejoin the class. This works, of course, only if you have relatively interesting lessons and exciting activities going on in the classroom, so that the misbehaving student would rather join in than remain in the time-out area.

As with a lot of what human beings tackle, the first time is the hardest. If we can get the misbehaving child to formulate one plan, even a simple plan as long as it works, we have set the stage for the next time and the next time after that.

5. Get a Commitment. Don't overlook this simple, yet important, step. Whether orally, or (better so) in writing, get a commitment. The sense of mutual trust that Reality Therapy is built upon increases the chance that plans for new behaviors will be carried out—after all we shook hands on it. One's word has been given. See the Chapter II suggestion, "*H* for Seal It with a *Handshake*," for more information on this point.

6. Accept No Excuses. Asking for excuses, encouraging excuses, listening to excuses, and accepting excuses are counterproductive. Excuses deal with the past. Glasser wants to deal with the future. If a plan for new behavior is not working, then either it must be re-examined to see how it can be made to work, *or* a new plan must be constructed. Our sights are ever forward—coming up with and successfully implementing a plan that does work. That is our collective goal. There is no place in Reality Therapy for accepting excuses. See the Chapter II suggestion, "*Y* for Don't Ask *Why*," for more information on excuses.

7. Don't Punish. Punishment lifts responsibility from the student's shoulders. If a plan for new behavior is broken, it cannot be fixed by punishing the student. Punishment, or even the threat of punishment, destroys the warmth, the trust, and the feeling that school is a good place—all so necessary for Reality Therapy to work. Remember how important it was in step two, identifying problem behavior, to have the student feel free of punishment in order to have him admit his wrongdoings? Further, punishment is a contrived consequence that when supplied bears little relationship to the misbehavior.

Is Glasser saying that students should suffer no consequences

for their misbehavior? No. Glasser would, as part of planning a
new behavior, see a place for supplying logical consequences —
those that are a logical result of the misbehavior. See the Chapter
II suggestion, "*C* for Consequences (Logical, Natural, *and*
Contrived)," for more information about punishment as a contrived consequence and about logical consequences.

8. Never Give Up — Be Persistent. How long is "never"? You decide.
   Glasser (1977, p. 61) offers a good basic rule of thumb: "hang in
   there longer than the student thinks you will."

REFERENCES

Brandt, R. (1988). On students' needs and team learning: A conversation
   with William Glasser. *Educational Leadership, 45*(6), 38–45. EJ
   370-222.

Glasser, W. (1969). *Schools without failure.* New York: Harper & Row.

Glasser, W. (1977). 10 steps to good discipline. *Today's Education, 66*(4),
   61–63. EJ 180-336.

Glasser, W. (1986). *Control theory in the classroom.* New York: Harper &
   Row.

Gough, P. (1987). The key to improving schools: An interview with
   William Glasser. *Phi Delta Kappan, 68*(9), 656–662. EJ 352-313.

Raffini, J. (1980). *Discipline: Negotiating conflicts with today's kids.* Englewood Cliffs, NJ: Prentice-Hall, Inc.

Note: The EJ number (for example, EJ 306-689) that follows each journal article can be used,
   in conjunction with the ERIC system described in Chapter IV, to obtain a copy of
   that article.

NONVERBAL COMMUNICATION OF AUTHORITY

*All Things Being Equal, What You Look or Sound Like
Influences Your Classroom Management*
C. S. Mester

All things being equal, what a teacher looks or sounds like can have a
significant effect upon his/her need to discipline and his/her ability to do
so successfully when needed. Since discipline in large part depends upon
the students' perception of the teacher's authority, those visible and
audible factors which impact upon one's image of authority deserve some
consideration. Scholars have long recognized that any speaker's establish-
ment of authority (or *ethos*) can be traced principally to listener perceptions based on the speaker's nonverbal behaviors.

Nonverbal behaviors include a plethora of vocal and physical expressions not all of which are completely within the speaker's conscious control. It follows then that if a teacher wishes to convey an authoritative image, he/she had best give some attention to his/her subconscious nonverbal messages in addition to making some conscious decisions about specific nonverbal symbols.

Against that background, let us examine the nonverbal components of image.

APPEARANCE

The most obvious nonverbal factor to consider is simply a teacher's physical appearance in terms of size, shape, and dress. Naturally, our size and shape are essentially beyond our control. But realizing what impact, if any, our size and shape might have upon our students' perceptions of our authority could move us to make compensatory adjustments in other nonverbal messages over which we can exercise control. The question of appearance then is two-fold: "Do I have to look like Lyle Alzado to command authority in my class?" and, if yes, "What can I do to get those results without taking up strength training?"

Lyle Alzado and his colleagues in pro football's front line would have a certain advantage in most classrooms simply because of their intimidating size. That advantage would only last as long as they exhibited the ability to earn their students' continuing respect through effective teaching strategies, however. Students can look up to a teacher of any stature. But many shorter teachers report that they feel more in control of the classroom and find it easier to gain students' initial respect if they stand while the students sit—thus encouraging the students to "look up" to them from the start.

Likewise, our manner of dress may make us feel and therefore be perceived as more authoritative. The beginning teacher who would like to have a little more self-confidence may be more comfortable in more formal attire than that preferred by the veteran teacher of established reputation. Business leaders encourage young people entering the profession to "dress for success." The same admonition applies to teachers even though our "dress" may come from Sears instead of Saks. The female teacher, then, may feel more authoritative when wearing a dress or suit than when wearing a slacks and sweater outfit. Similarly, the male teacher may convey a more authoritative manner when wearing a necktie instead of the more casual open-necked shirt. Since how we feel about ourselves directly influences how others perceive us, our clothing choices should complement a positive, authoritative self-image.

The issue of dressing to establish an image of authority may be especially important for teachers of the primary grades whose students are still learning the important role relationships in the classroom setting. For instance, comments of young Catholic schoolchildren indicate a certain preference for teaching nuns who wear a habit of some version. Their preference derives from the sense of comfort they experience in knowing — by the "uniform" — who is in charge. By the habit-garbed nun's very appearance, they know who she is and what behaviors she expects of them. That security is clearly connected to the broad issue of discipline in the elementary schools.

Closely related to the issue of dress are a teacher's personal grooming habits. Since a neat and clean-looking speaker engenders a greater sense of respect among listeners, a well-groomed teacher has a better chance of maintaining order in the classroom than an unkempt teacher. One can be neat and clean within a broad range of personal grooming styles, so one's individual style need not be sacrificed.

To the extent, then, that a teacher's ability to maintain order in the classroom is related to that teacher's self-confidence and first impression with the students, appearance is a factor for the teacher's consideration. Appearance includes size, shape, grooming, and manner of dress.

VOICE

To establish that the sound of a speaker's voice has an impact on his/her perceived authority, one need only look to the history of broadcasting. For decades, women were not considered for on-air news reporting because their voices didn't "sound authoritative enough." The factors their voices seemed to lack (according to network executives) were a low pitch and a firm tone — factors perceived to convey trustworthiness and expertise. Gradually, that situation has changed. More and more women are serving as news anchorpersons and are being well received by the public. But, still and all, to be hired for such positions, an applicant of either gender needs a voice that is well modulated and has a capacity for firmness. Such vocal qualities convey sufficient authority to make the news report credible. Teachers have a comparable need to sound credible.

Like the newscaster, a teacher whose voice is well modulated is easier to listen to than one whose voice is flat or expressionless. Therefore, the teacher with the stronger voice should have less occasion to discipline students for inattentiveness. Further, the teacher whose voice is reasonably firm will be more believable when correcting or warning students. As former students ourselves, we have all probably suffered through a class taught by a monotonous, boring professor. That experience ought to have taught us that students are not always the guilty parties when their behavior is undesirable.

To be effective vocally, then, a teacher needs to have sufficient vocal variety in pitch, volume, and rate to give diversity and dimension to the expression of ideas. Varied expression appropriate to the classroom does not need to be melodramatic but just inflected enough to hold students' attention through even the warmest spring afternoon. Vocal variety is a greater asset to classroom discipline than is vocal power. The teacher should not need to boom or shout in order to maintain a supportive classroom atmosphere. If some students in our class are being disruptive, we can get their attention by stopping our own talk and staring at the offender or by continuing our talk in a hushed tone. Either strategy is actually more effective than shouting them down. More important than that particular tip is the general premise that our voices should reflect our own enthusiasm for our subject. Follow that general rule, and your students will catch your enthusiasm instead of diminishing it.

GESTURE AND MOVEMENT

As with voice, the best kind of gesture and movement for a teacher to use is that which is varied according to the particular nature of the ideas being discussed and the setting in which the discussion occurs. So there is no single right way to move or gesture while conducting class. Each room has its own special constraints and possibilities that affect the teacher's movement choices.

A few simple guidelines can be noted, however, that may enhance classroom atmosphere and reduce the need for discipline. Primary among these guidelines is direct eye contact. In order to cause a student to realize that we are earnest in our wish to get his/her attention, and, hence, to have a chance to modify behavior, we must be looking that student squarely in the eyes. The old-timer's admonition to the young, "never trust a man who won't look you in the eye," is well grounded in the reality of interpersonal relationships. Such contact individualizes the teacher/student relationship and strengthens the bond of trust enabling the learning process and the discipline that may be involved. So no matter what the physical obstacles a particular classroom presents, a teacher should work around them to establish direct eye contact with students—particularly when engaged in discipline.

A second guideline for appropriate physical expression when trying to establish an authoritative image is the principle of forward motion. That is, an individual is perceived as unintimidated by an audience if he/she does not physically back up when asked a question or challenged. The principle certainly applies to the classroom teacher. By backing up, the teacher may inadvertently imply to the students that they have the balance of power in the classroom. To put the suggestion in the positive, a teacher will convey a comparatively authoritative image by standing firm or moving slightly forward when asked a challenging question. Such a posture shows respect for the question and questioner as well as sufficient self-confidence to deal with that challenge. Mutual respect again reduces the need for discipline and increases its chances of success when necessary.

Finally a teacher's movement can be a factor that encourages student attentiveness and interest, thus diminishing misbehavior. Like any good public speaker, a teacher should speak with sufficient animation to give life and flavor to ideas without becoming distractingly active. Gesture, facial expression, and total body movement need to be consistent with the subject matter and the level of the audience's interest and knowledge relative to the subject. Our movements should be purposeful and clear, not frantic or nervous. As with a firm vocal expression, a firm manner of gesturing conveys our expertise and earnestness. Our movement and gesture should say to students that this subject matter is interesting, perhaps even fascinating. Such a nonverbal message in combination with a compatible verbal message will create a stimulating, nondisruptive classroom atmosphere.

SUMMARY

Much of our nonverbal expression is a result of our individual personality and background. In spite of that, nonverbal messages can be consciously controlled and frequently should be, since they have a very significant effect on our image as speakers. This general truth is particularly pertinent to the teacher whose overall success is dependent on conveying a positive self-image and maintaining order in the classroom.

Note: C. S. Mester is an instructor in Speech Communication at the Behrend College of Penn State University, Erie, PA. She has over twenty years teaching experience.

Educational Resources Information Center (ERIC)

ERIC: THE INFORMATION "GENIE" FOR EDUCATORS

How many of you have your own copy of Grossnickle and Sesko's (1985) seventy-nine page guide "Promoting Effective Discipline in School and Classroom: A Practitioner's Perspective"? Just a few of you. Too bad. Well, how many had the opportunity personally to hear the speech given on "Disciplinary Techniques Reported by Parents of Gifted Children," delivered at the Western Psychological Association Conference in San Jose, California, a couple of years ago? Couldn't get the time off? No money in the travel budget? That's a real shame. Did you read the 1986 *Phi Delta Kappan* five-page article titled "A Primer on Classroom Discipline: Principles Old and New"? That journal isn't in your school's professional library? That's a shame. All three of these resources, and *thousands* more, could be a real help in establishing and maintaining classroom discipline.

Returning to reality, most faculty, busy with teaching responsibilities and on limited travel budgets, do not have the time or resources to attend as many professional meetings as they would like. Further, even the best of reports, conference proceedings, and curriculum guides generally have a rather limited distribution—often only to participants. Busy educators also have limited time to scan the literature, even the limited literature available to them, looking for "just the right article" to help them. Yet, for the classroom teacher, information gained through such sources could serve as the basis for establishing, maintaining, and/or improving their classroom management.

What kinds of topics related to classroom management might teachers have a need to know more about? Just for starters, how about "delinquency," "suspensions," "due process," "child abuse," "academic vs. nonacademic penalties for misconduct," "legal issues," "gifted children," "handicapped children," "school size and school disorder," "discipline in foreign countries," "beginning teachers' guides to discipline," "managing classroom conflict," "assessment of classroom problems," "influence of families," "change strategies," "assertiveness training," "behavior modification," "first-year teacher survival," "punishment," "medicine and discipline," "disciplinary hearings," "knowledge of legally sanctioned discipline procedures," and "gender and corporal punishment." The topics are almost endless, each demanding quality information before precious time, effort, and resources are committed.

Wouldn't it be great if it were possible quickly and easily to access, at minimal cost, conference proceedings, curriculum or instructor guides, opinion papers, bibliographies, descriptive or research reports, program evaluations, journal articles, speeches, or test/questionnaires in education? You might be thinking that while you are wishing, you may as well wish for a brand new lab, more motivated students, and . . . a 45-foot sailing yacht! Send in the bottle with the genie!

All of these sources of information, in fact, are currently available through a system called ERIC. It is even better than a bottle with a genie in it. A genie only grants three wishes; ERIC grants an unlimited number of requests for information. It is one of the most widely searched and heavily used bibliographic data bases in the world today. ERIC resources are used more than 1.7 million times annually, providing users with more than 30 million bibliographic and/or primary documents (ERIC Clearinghouse on Information Resources 1985) Yet, for some reason, ERIC has too often been kept a secret from practitioners.

What Is ERIC?

ERIC, an acronym for Educational Resources Information Center, is a twenty-year-old, worldwide-available information system. It is sponsored by the National Institute of Education, within the U.S. Department of Education. It is dedicated to the progress of education through the dissemination of education research results, PRACTITIONER-RELATED materials, and other resource information that can be used in developing more effective educational programs. Being decentralized, it is composed of sixteen clearinghouses, each responsible for obtaining, evaluating, abstracting, and disseminating information in a specific field of education. The sixteen clearinghouses are listed in Appendix I.

Access to ERIC

Access to ERIC materials is made through one of two indexes, *Resources in Education* (RIE) and *Current Index to Journals in Education* (CIJE). The indexes are available in most college or university libraries, state departments of education, larger school districts, and some public libraries.

Resources in Education (RIE)

As with the "R" in ERIC, the "R" in RIE stands for Resources, not Research. This is an especially important point for those who might dismiss ERIC as being useful only for researchers, not practitioners. RIE is a monthly journal that abstracts, indexes, announces, and provides a procedure to access "fugitive" documents. These documents, such as conference proceedings, speeches, curriculum guides, and project reports, are not normally available through library channels. Prior to RIE, the only way one was aware of such documents was to have personally attended the conference, heard the speech, or to have known someone who had an extra copy of the desired curriculum guide or report. This hit-or-miss process severely limited one's access to information in the past. Not so now!

To use RIE, the first step is to look up the topic in the SUBJECT INDEX or AUTHOR INDEX. Once an appropriate title is identified (for example, "Career Planning for Women") make note of the accompanying six-digit identifying "ED" (ERIC Document) number. In this instance, the number would be ED 654-321. Documents are also catalogued by INSTITUTION and PUBLICATION TYPE. As titles can often be misleading, the second step is to turn to the RESUME portion of the same index, use the six-digit "ED" number, and locate the RESUME (detailed abstract).

As it shows in the SAMPLE RESUME (Appendix II), much information is provided, including: author, origination of the document, publication type, descriptive note, key descriptors, and, *most importantly,* a rather lengthy informative abstract. Content experts at ERIC clearinghouses actually read each document in order to prepare these abstracts. This saves users like you and me a whole lot of time, effort, and possibly disappointment in ordering something that ends up being nothing like what we thought it was going to be. Often the detailed abstracts alone contain enough information to help make decisions.

If an identified document appears to be just what you are looking for, follow the simple directions provided in the RIE index to secure a microfiche (or paper) copy of the entire document. Note, if microfiche are obtained directly from ERIC, they cost about $0.97 per microfiche, each of which can hold up to ninety-six pages of print. A more common method of getting a desired document on microfiche is to obtain it from a government-sponsored ERIC microfiche collection depository (usually based at, or at least available through college/university libraries). These microfiche collections ensure that a document will never go out of print.

RIE documents go through a quality screening process by reviewers who, typically, have terminal degrees in their field and have experience with ERIC of a decade or more. They apply selection standards similar to those used for refereed journals in order to decide what is worth announcing in RIE. The fact that ERIC's RIE is used by approximately 190,000 people per week and that three out of every four educators cite what they receive as being "very useful" testifies to the success of the screening process (see *How to Use ERIC* 1979, under "Resource Publications," p. 147).

To whet your curiosity about what you can locate in RIE on the topic discipline, I have prepared a sampling of documents; you will find these sample documents in Appendix IV. These and many other documents are easily retrievable through ERIC's *Resources in Education.*

Current Index to Journals in Education (CIJE)

CIJE includes articles from over 750 education periodicals, ranging from the most popular United States' practitioner-oriented journals to British, Canadian, and Australian journals. It abstracts, indexes, announces, and provides access to these journal articles. It is like having an enormous library right at your fingertips!

To use CIJE, first look up the topic in the SUBJECT INDEX. Upon identifying an appropriate article, note its title, the journal in which it appears (name, volume, number, page), and the six-digit "EJ" (ERIC Journal) number. The same information could be located by scanning CIJE's AUTHOR INDEX or JOURNAL CONTENTS INDEX. Using the latter is like walking up and down the aisles of a very large library, opening desired journals to examine their Tables of Contents.

As with the titles of RIE documents, the titles of journal articles do not always convey the real content of the articles. Why waste your time requesting and securing articles that may not be of use? Instead, note the six-digit "EJ" number, turn to the MAIN ENTRY section, and locate the corresponding abstract (see Appendix III for a sample CIJE MAIN ENTRY abstract). Key information displayed includes a repeat of the article title and journal name, as well as author, KEY DESCRIPTORS, and a one- or two-sentence abstract.

This additional information, although considerably less than what is included in RIE abstracts, often clarifies whether or not an article is worth obtaining. Selected articles are usually accessible from nearby college libraries. If not, by using the "EJ" number and the Article Copy Service address in the CIJE index, you can quickly obtain them directly from ERIC. No resource is very far beyond your reach!

The quality of articles identified and accessed through CIJE is ensured by the referee process inherent in most journal selection procedures. Users apparently agree, as approximately 140,000 people use CIJE each week, with three out of every five reporting success in finding sought-after information (see *How to Use ERIC* 1979, under "Resource Publications," p. 147).

To whet your curiosity, once again, about what you can locate in CIJE on the topic discipline, I have prepared a sampling of journal articles. You will find these sample journal articles in Appendix V. Note how many different journals publish articles on the topic of classroom management. These and many other articles are easily retrievable through ERIC's *Current Index to Journals in Education.*

Thesaurus of ERIC Descriptors

One difficulty some busy practitioners have when "looking up" information is that they call what they are looking for one thing and the index they are using calls it something else. To alleviate this problem, ERIC publishes a *Thesaurus of ERIC Descriptors.* It is normally found on the reference shelf just next to the RIE and CIJE indexes. The *Thesaurus* is a controlled vocabulary of educational terms called descriptors. They are used to index and enter documents into the ERIC system *and to assist users in searching the system.* A user might look up "discipline" only to find descriptors including "disciplinary actions," "discipline," "discipline policy," and "discipline problems."

Most often each of the descriptors will list RELATED TERMS. For instance, "discipline" refers the reader to, among other descriptors, "behavior problems," "classroom techniques," "corporal punishment," "obedience," "punishment," "sanctions," and "self control." In turn, each of these RELATED TERMS would refer the user to the descriptor "discipline." A couple of minutes' work with the *Thesaurus* pays great dividends when undertaking a search for information.

Computer Search Capability: Information on a SilverPlatter™

Thus far, what has been described is a hand search of the two ERIC indexes, a process available to all educators. One can also conduct a computer search of ERIC, entering key descriptors and allowing the computer to do the clerical work of locating and then sorting through documents.

One such commonly available computerized system for searching ERIC is called SilverPlatter. It literally provides the user with information on a silver platter, or in our case, on a CD or compact disk. To access all of ERIC, from 1966, several compact disks are required. A SilverPlatter CD looks just like those shiny compact disks that are so popular in today's music world. Each SilverPlatter CD is linked to a microcomputer.

To search ERIC on SilverPlatter, one simply enters (types) a key descriptor or descriptors, previews the located citations, and then prints any interesting citations found during the search. If a descriptor is entered with a dash immediately following (for example, discipline-), SilverPlatter will search for that word as a formal descriptor. If that same term is entered without the dash (for example, discipline), SilverPlatter will search for the word anywhere in the record.

The real power of a computerized search comes when one combines descriptors. For instance, if one entered the descriptor, HANDICAPPED, one would find 5895 citations (1983–1988) containing that term somewhere in the total record. If one entered the descriptor, PUNISHMENT-, one would generate 170 citations containing that term as a formal descriptor. If one entered the descriptors, HANDICAPPED *and* PUNISHMENT-, in seconds the computer would conduct a sort revealing nine citations— most likely just what you were looking for.

Try to imagine how long it would have taken to do such a search by hand. Try to imagine how long it would take to do a hand search combining the descriptors, KINDERGARTEN *or* EARLY-CHILDHOOD, POSITIVE REINFORCEMENT, HANDICAPPED, TEACHERS *or* TEACHING. ERIC on SilverPlatter can do it in a matter of seconds!

Where do you find ERIC on SilverPlatter? Probably right around the corner. More and more colleges and universities have (or soon will have) this service available. There are over one thousand institutions worldwide subscribing to ERIC on SilverPlatter. Little or no computer literacy is needed. Be prepared for the time to fly right by before you know it. It is easy to get caught up in the thrill, *yes thrill,* of being able to unlock just the information you want quickly. It is actually fun!

The end result of your efforts will be an on-target bibliography, complete with abstracts, if you so desire. Whether doing a hand search or a SilverPlatter computerized search, you will be more successful if, while looking for information, you use the same terminology by which ERIC clearinghouse personnel have initially catalogued it.

Warning! Prepare a "Shopping List"

Most people know what happens when they are hungry and go grocery shopping without a list. They come home with a lot more than what they went for. The same is true when an information-"hungry" person uses ERIC's RIE or CIJE. As you scan an ERIC SUBJECT INDEX, you end up spotting interesting and useful resources outside your primary area of investigation. If you want to avoid this situation, prepare an investigation "shopping list" beforehand. Then again, why not let your imagination and your newfound information retrieval system run wild?

Publish, Who Me?

Who are these people who publish in ERIC, especially in RIE? Who designs the curriculum guides, the tests, and the follow-up questionnaires announced in RIE? Who conducts and then writes up the successful projects that are reported; and who describes the workings of the general advisory committees? People just like you publish in ERIC. In most schools, exciting things are happening that really ought to be shared. ERIC's RIE is just the vehicle for that sharing. The simple guidelines for doing this are described in *Submitting Documents to ERIC,* listed below under "Resource Publications."

CONCLUSION

There is simply not enough space in an article this length to describe fully the workings of ERIC and its potential to serve educators. What I had hoped to do is spark your interest in using ERIC as a tool to acquire the information so often requisite to successful problem solving. Quite bluntly, no other single information cataloging, indexing, and retrieval source exists that can match ERIC. Just as students are taught how important it is to possess the proper "tools of the trade" before tackling a job, it is equally important for educators to do the same. For educators facing problem situations, the "tools of the trade" means being able quickly to access useful information.

As a concerned educator, consider scheduling (or asking to have scheduled) an in-service program on ERIC. Acquire copies of the following resource publications, identify the closest library having the RIE and CIJE indexes, and clarify the specific process faculty would use to acquire microfiche and/or paper copies of requested information. Pick out a problem in education, and put ERIC, the information genie, to work for you.

RESOURCE PUBLICATIONS

Whether you choose to use ERIC or, even better, you decide to lead your institution in that direction, additional information would be helpful. The publications listed below are available, free of charge, from ERIC Processing and Reference Facility, 4350 East-West Highway, Suite 1100, Bethesda, Maryland 20814-4475. They include:

> *A Pocket Guide to ERIC*
> *Submitting Documents to ERIC*
> *Directory of ERIC Microfiche Collections*
> *Directory of ERIC Search Services*
> *How to Use ERIC*

Another source, *All About ERIC,* is available from the U.S. Government Printing Office, Washington, DC 20402. This thirty-one–page pamphlet not only describes the operation of ERIC's clearinghouses, RIE, and CIJE, but also identifies several low-cost, color videocassette and film-strip audiocassette programs that could be used for an in-service program on ERIC.

REFERENCES

ERIC Clearinghouse on Information Resources. (1985, December). *ERIC DIGEST: ERIC for Practitioners.*

U.S. Government Printing Office. (1979, December). *How to Use ERIC,* p. 19.

Note: The first two resources cited in the opening paragraph of Chapter IV are accessible through ERIC's RIE, using document numbers ED 266-550 and ED 260-572, respectively. The third resource cited, the article in *Phi Delta Kappan,* is accessible either through a local college/university library or through ERIC's CIJE, using document number EJ 341-137.

APPENDIX I

Adult, Career, & Vocational
Ohio State University
Center for Research in Vocational Ed.
1960 Kenny Road
Columbus, Ohio 43210-1090
(614) 292-4353

Counseling and Personnel Services
University of Michigan
School of Education, Room 2108
610 East University Street
Ann Arbor, Michigan 48109-1259
(313) 764-9492

Educational Management
University of Oregon
1787 Agate Street
Eugene, Oregon 97403-5207
(503) 686-5043

Elementary and Early Childhood
University of Illinois
805 W. Pennsylvania Avenue
Urbana, Illinois 61801-4897
(217) 333-1386

Handicapped and Gifted Children
Council for Exceptional Children
1920 Association Drive
Reston, Virginia 22091-1589
(703) 620-3660

Higher Education
George Washington University
One Dupont Circle, N.W., Suite 630
Washington, DC 20036-1183
(202) 296-2597

Information Resources
Syracuse University
Huntington Hall, Room 030
150 Marshall Street
Syracuse, New York 13244-2340
(315) 443-3640

Junior Colleges
University of California at Los Angeles
Mathematical Sciences Bldg., Rm. 8118
405 Hilgard Avenue
Los Angeles, California 90024-1564
(213) 825-3931

Languages and Linguistics
Center for Applied Linguistics
1118 22nd St., N.W.
Washington, DC 20037-0037
(202) 429-9551

Sixteen ERIC Clearinghouses

Reading and Communication Skills
Indiana University
Smith Research Center, Suite 150
2805 East 10th Street
Bloomington, Indiana 47408-2373
(812) 335-5847

Rural Education and Small Schools
Appalachia Educational Laboratory
1031 Quarrier Street
P.O. Box 1348
Charleston, West Virginia 25325-1348
(304) 347-0400

Science, Mathematics,
  & Environmental Ed.
Ohio State University
1200 Chambers Road, Room 310
Columbus, Ohio 43212-1792
(614) 292-6717

Social Studies/Social Science
Indiana University
Social Studies Devel. Center,
  Suite 120
2805 East 10th Street
Bloomington, Indiana 47405-2373
(812) 335-3838

Teacher Education
American Assoc. Colleges for
  Teacher Ed.
One Dupont Circle, N.W., Suite 610
Washington, DC 20036-2412
(202) 293-2450

Tests, Measurement, and Evaluation
American Institutes for Research
Washington Research Center
3333 Kaye N.W., Suite 300
Washington, DC 20007-3893
(202) 342-5000

Urban Education
Teachers College, Columbia
  University
Institute for Urban and Minority Ed.
Main Hall, Room 300, Box 40
525 West 120th Street
New York, New York 10027-9998
(212) 678-3433

APPENDIX II
RIE Document Résumé

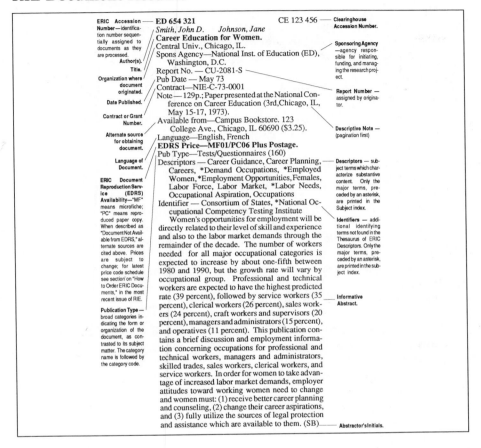

ERIC Accession Number—identification number sequentially assigned to documents as they are processed.

Author(s).

Title.

Organization where document originated.

Date Published.

Contract or Grant Number.

Alternate source for obtaining document.

Language of Document.

ERIC Document Reproduction Service (EDRS) Availability—"MF" means microfiche; "PC" means reproduced paper copy. When described as "Document Not Available from EDRS," alternate sources are cited above. Prices are subject to change; for latest price code schedule see section on "How to Order ERIC Documents," in the most recent issue of RIE.

Publication Type — broad categories indicating the form or organization of the document, as contrasted to its subject matter. The category name is followed by the category code.

ED 654 321   CE 123 456

Smith, John D.   Johnson, Jane
Career Education for Women.
Central Univ., Chicago, IL.
Spons Agency—National Inst. of Education (ED), Washington, D.C.
Report No. — CU-2081-S
Pub Date — May 73
Contract—NIE-C-73-0001
Note — 129p.; Paper presented at the National Conference on Career Education (3rd, Chicago, IL, May 15-17, 1973).
Available from—Campus Bookstore. 123 College Ave., Chicago, IL 60690 ($3.25).
Language—English, French
EDRS Price—MF01/PC06 Plus Postage.
Pub Type—Tests/Questionnaires (160)
Descriptors — Career Guidance, Career Planning, Careers, *Demand Occupations, *Employed Women, *Employment Opportunities, Females, Labor Force, Labor Market, *Labor Needs, Occupational Aspiration, Occupations
Identifier — Consortium of States, *National Occupational Competency Testing Institute

Women's opportunities for employment will be directly related to their level of skill and experience and also to the labor market demands through the remainder of the decade. The number of workers needed for all major occupational categories is expected to increase by about one-fifth between 1980 and 1990, but the growth rate will vary by occupational group. Professional and technical workers are expected to have the highest predicted rate (39 percent), followed by service workers (35 percent), clerical workers (26 percent), sales workers (24 percent), craft workers and supervisors (20 percent), managers and administrators (15 percent), and operatives (11 percent). This publication contains a brief discussion and employment information concerning occupations for professional and technical workers, managers and administrators, skilled trades, sales workers, clerical workers, and service workers. In order for women to take advantage of increased labor market demands, employer attitudes toward working women need to change and women must: (1) receive better career planning and counseling, (2) change their career aspirations, and (3) fully utilize the sources of legal protection and assistance which are available to them. (SB)

Clearinghouse Accession Number.

Sponsoring Agency —agency responsible for initiating, funding, and managing the research project.

Report Number — assigned by originator.

Descriptive Note — (pagination first)

Descriptors — subject terms which characterize substantive content. Only the major terms, preceded by an asterisk, are printed in the Subject index.

Identifiers — additional identifying terms not found in the Thesaurus of ERIC Descriptors. Only the major terms, preceded by an asterisk, are printed in the subject index.

Informative Abstract.

Abstractor's Initials.

APPENDIX III
CIJE Journal Abstracts

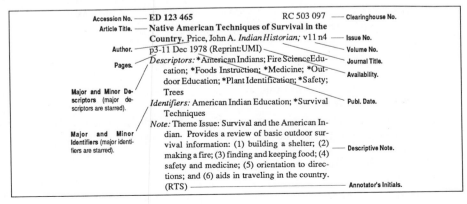

Accession No. — **ED 123 465**   RC 503 097

Article Title. — **Native American Techniques of Survival in the Country.** Price, John A. *Indian Historian;* v11 n4
Author. — p3-11 Dec 1978 (Reprint:UMI)
Pages.
Descriptors: *American Indians; Fire Science Education; *Foods Instruction; *Medicine; *Outdoor Education; *Plant Identification; *Safety; Trees
Identifiers: American Indian Education; *Survival Techniques
Note: Theme Issue: Survival and the American Indian. Provides a review of basic outdoor survival information: (1) building a shelter; (2) making a fire; (3) finding and keeping food; (4) safety and medicine; (5) orientation to directions; and (6) aids in traveling in the country. (RTS)

Clearinghouse No.

Issue No.

Volume No.

Journal Title.

Availability.

Publ. Date.

Major and Minor Descriptors (major descriptors are starred).

Major and Minor Identifiers (major identifiers are starred).

Descriptive Note.

Annotator's Initials.

APPENDIX IV
RIE Sample Résumés on Discipline — Just to Tease You

The selections below represent only a very small fraction of the many curriculum guides, research reports, speeches, conference proceedings, and other reference materials that exist on discipline. All of these, and more, are easily retrievable through ERIC!

ED 268-646
Creative behavior modification strategies that work.

ED 261-002
Classroom management: Teacher/assistant teacher staff development materials.

ED 263-659
Knowledge of legally sanctioned discipline procedures by school personnel.

ED 265-939
Kindergarten children's perceptions of classroom rules.

ED 270-062
Medicine handbook.

ED 250-784
A blueprint for classroom discipline. Action kit no. 3.

ED 259-829
Fostering discipline: Instructor's manual.

ED 250-762
1001 alternatives to corporal punishment. A practical handbook of outrageous, original, and sometimes useful ideas.

ED 252-926
School discipline policy: A problem of balance.

ED 240-058
A positive approach to assertive discipline.

ED 241-993
Student discipline programs that work.

ED 241-995
Student discipline and public law 94-142.

ED 234-013
What do you do when . . . ? A handbook for classroom discipline problems with practical and positive solutions.

ED 265-945
Parents and teachers as discipline shapers.

ED 218-711
Preventative classroom management.

ED 253-523
The development of classroom management workshops through an in-service training program.

ED 253-529
Discipline strategies for teachers of problem students.

ED 218-713
Training teachers to be effective classroom managers.

APPENDIX V

CIJE Sample Abstracts on Discipline — Just to Tease You Some More

Note the variety of journals with an interest in discipline. *All* of these articles, and many, many more, are available to you through your local college library or directly through ERIC. Nothing is out of your reach!

EJ 372-018
 NASSP Bulletin, 67(5), 36–37, 1988
 The boy who couldn't be disciplined.

EJ 347-878
 Rural Educator, 8(1), 16–21, 1986
 Rural principal: A case study of an effective disciplinarian.

EJ 348-367
 Instructor, 96(7), 16–19, 1987
 It's time we stop paddling kids.

EJ 301-000
 Educational Horizons, 92(4), 129–131, 1984
 A major source of discipline problems: Miscalls.

EJ 298-008
 NASSP Bulletin, 68(471), 74–79, 1984
 Discipline in middle school—Parent, teacher, and principal concerns.

EJ 299-546
 Educational Leadership, 41(8), 75–76, 1984
 High standards for effective discipline.

EJ 375-659
 Learning, 16(9), 38–40, 1988
 Nothing was ever Timothy's fault.

EJ 323-546
 Principal, 63(4), 44–46, 1985
 The positive view of discipline: How three teachers do it.

EJ 336-311
 Momentum, 17(2), 20–21, 1986
 School discipline: Better to be loved or feared?

EJ 325-667
 Education Canada, 25(3), 29, 1985
 The discipline situation: Some possible solutions.

EJ 329-619
 School Law Bulletin, 16(4), 18–28, 1985
 Academic penalties for misconduct and nonattendance.

EJ 322-930
 Instructor, 95(2), 125, 1985
 Troubleshooters' guide to classroom discipline.

EJ 320-916
 English Journal, 74(5), 40–42, 1985
 Writing as punishment.

EJ 318-845
> *Small School Forum,* 6(2), 13–16, 1985
> School discipline: A review.

EJ 375-657
> *Learning,* 16(9), 12–13, 1988
> Put away the paddle—forever.

EJ 312-679
> *Science Teacher,* 52(1), 38–40, 1985
> Friendly persuasion.

EJ 314-601
> *Jr of Phys Ed, Recreation & Dance,* 56(2), 29–30, 1985
> Handling problems in discipline: Guidelines for success.

EJ 314-217
> *Young Children,* 40(3), 47–52, 1985
> Building self-control: Discipline for young children.

EJ 306-692
> *Phi Delta Kappan,* 66(1), 53–54, 1985
> Calm discipline.

EJ 309-989
> *American School Board Journal,* 172(1), 45–46, 1985
> Follow these six steps, and learn to manage student misbehavior.

EJ 370-179
> *The Clearing House,* 61(8), 356–357, 1988
> Effective teaching techniques: Implications for better discipline.

EJ 369-760
> *Urban Education,* 22(4), 476–495, 1988
> Alternatives to suspension and corporal punishment.